CW01302207

Palgrave Studies in European Union Politics

Series Editors
Michelle Egan, American University, Washington, USA
William E. Paterson, Aston University, Birmingham, UK
Kolja Raube, KU Leuven, Leuven, Belgium

Following on the sustained success of the acclaimed European Union Series, which essentially publishes research-based textbooks, Palgrave Studies in European Union Politics publishes cutting edge research-driven monographs. The remit of the series is broadly defined, both in terms of subject and academic discipline. All topics of significance concerning the nature and operation of the European Union potentially fall within the scope of the series. The series is multidisciplinary to reflect the growing importance of the EU as a political, economic and social phenomenon. To submit a proposal, please contact Senior Editor Ambra Finotello ambra. finotello@palgrave.com.

This series is indexed by Scopus.

Editorial Board

Laurie Buonanno (SUNY Buffalo State, USA)
Kenneth Dyson (Cardiff University, UK)
Brigid Laffan (European University Institute, Italy)
Claudio Radaelli (University College London, UK)
Mark Rhinard (Stockholm University, Sweden)
Ariadna Ripoll Servent (University of Bamberg, Germany)
Frank Schimmelfennig (ETH Zurich, Switzerland)
Claudia Sternberg (University College London, UK)
Nathalie Tocci (Istituto Affari Internazionali, Italy)

Bernhard Weßels · Richard Rose

European Public Opinion about Security

Who Can Help Us in a Threatening World?

palgrave macmillan

Bernhard Weßels
Social Science Research Center Berlin
Berlin, Germany

Richard Rose
Centre for the Study of Public Policy
University of Strathclyde
Glasgow, UK

ISSN 2662-5873 ISSN 2662-5881 (electronic)
Palgrave Studies in European Union Politics
ISBN 978-3-031-86262-5 ISBN 978-3-031-86263-2 (eBook)
https://doi.org/10.1007/978-3-031-86263-2

© The Editor(s) (if applicable) and The Author(s), under exclusive license to Springer Nature Switzerland AG 2025

This work is subject to copyright. All rights are solely and exclusively licensed by the Publisher, whether the whole or part of the material is concerned, specifically the rights of translation, reprinting, reuse of illustrations, recitation, broadcasting, reproduction on microfilms or in any other physical way, and transmission or information storage and retrieval, electronic adaptation, computer software, or by similar or dissimilar methodology now known or hereafter developed.
The use of general descriptive names, registered names, trademarks, service marks, etc. in this publication does not imply, even in the absence of a specific statement, that such names are exempt from the relevant protective laws and regulations and therefore free for general use.
The publisher, the authors and the editors are safe to assume that the advice and information in this book are believed to be true and accurate at the date of publication. Neither the publisher nor the authors or the editors give a warranty, expressed or implied, with respect to the material contained herein or for any errors or omissions that may have been made. The publisher remains neutral with regard to jurisdictional claims in published maps and institutional affiliations.

Cover illustration: © Harvey Loake

This Palgrave Macmillan imprint is published by the registered company Springer Nature Switzerland AG
The registered company address is: Gewerbestrasse 11, 6330 Cham, Switzerland

If disposing of this product, please recycle the paper.

Introduction

Multiple Threats and Multiple Allies

Europeans today are threatened by insecurity in many forms. There are threats from the global economy, from military aggression and from climate change. Dealing with security threats calls for action by government, since protecting national security is one of its primary responsibilities. When threats come from abroad, a national government must take into account what other countries do. A government can respond on its own or join an alliance to address a threat common to many countries. Depending on the type of threat, it may look for help to the European Union, to NATO or to the United Nations. A big majority of European states belong to all three of these institutions.

Threats to national security put pressure on the government to adopt policies that have significant costs. This makes politicians hesitant to publicise threats until a crisis is very visible. In response to the war in Ukraine, the United States is putting pressure on European allies to meet their formal obligation to spend more money on defence. The European Central Bank tries to reduce the effect of global inflation by raising interest rates that increase the cost of living and constrain economic growth. Adapting to climate change has big up-front costs to reduce carbon emissions and generate renewable resources, while benefits may take decades to show up. Doing nothing also has costs if inflation persists, if Russia weaponises access to energy, and if climate change creates more extreme heat waves every few years.

Every European government has limited resources to protect security on its own. The median European country's population of fewer than 10 million people places a low ceiling on the size of its military force by comparison with Russia, with a population 14 times larger. Whatever its per capita income, the total size of a country's Gross Domestic Product is limited by its population. Thus, a county such as Denmark has a total GDP much less than that of Poland, because Poland's population is six times larger than Denmark.

National governments have a choice of alliances to increase their security; the European Union is only one potential ally. Hence, this book goes beyond a narrow focus on what is done in Brussels to consider the priority European governments give to NATO for military defence and to the United Nations for dealing with climate change. If no ally is considered suitable, a country may deal with a security challenge on its own.

Because European governments are democratically accountable, they must maintain the support of their citizens for decisions that have major consequences. Relying on the European Central Bank (ECB) to deal with inflation can cost a government votes if the ECB adopts a policy that imposes austerity on the eurozone. Given a cultural aversion to military force following defeat in the Second World War, the German government has been slow to mobilise an increased military force, notwithstanding the statement of the Federal Chancellor that Russia's invasion of Ukraine was a turning point. Dealing with the threat of climate change is politically complicated if it involves policies that require its electorate to reduce use of their car and make expensive alterations to heating their home.

The Book's Aim

Our purpose is to find out whether Europeans see their country facing multiple threats to their security today and if so, do they want their government to deal with threats on their own or get help from the European Union, the UN or NATO? We answer these questions by analysing data from the eight-nation European Security Survey of public opinion. Given substantial differences about security, we test whether people differ in their views due to their political attitudes and social characteristics; their national context; or because of differences between threats and alliances. The results have important implications for the European Union, for Europeans and for democratic governments.

We live in a time of polycrisis with many threats to security. Chapter 1 distinguishes how these threats have evolved historically. Military threats have developed from massing foot soldiers to massing drones and cyber attacks. Threats to the economy were once confined to conflicts between hungry urban residents and farmers who produced food. The development of a global economy has created a political economy in which China is now seen as a source of risk as well as cheap imported goods. When growing populations began clustering in cities this threatened public health and the response was public sanitation. The growth in manufacturing and new life styles have combined to change the climate with potentially dire future consequences.

The impact of security threats is variable. An aggressive attack by a foreign army threatens the territory and lives of all the people living within its path. The global economy has tended to increase prosperity, albeit in cycles in which economic growth raises incomes unequally while inflation hits all consumers. Climate insecurity affects the whole of a country's population, but the form differs depending on proximity to flood risks or being farmers affected by changes in the weather.

For each threat democratic governments have a choice between remaining exclusively accountable to their voters or joining a multi-national alliance to increase the effectiveness of policies while becoming accountable to alliance partners too. Immediately after the Second World War European elites began creating multi-national alliances offering a more effective means of maintaining security than before. Elites relied on an increasingly prosperous and secure public supporting the extension of their protection from their national capital to Brussels and Washington.

A national government's choice of allies tends to differ with the type of threat. Chapter 2 describes the distinctive characteristics of multi-national alliances and their comparative advantages and limitations. The European Union seeks to provide economic security through the European Central Bank and economic growth through the Single European Market. The EU now has a High Representative for Foreign Affairs and Security Policy promoting strategic autonomy policies intended to reduce dependence on decisions taken by the American president. However, its military capacity is limited because of the lack of a European army.

The North Atlantic Treaty Organization (NATO) enhances the military effectiveness of European states by magnitudes. Article 5 of the NATO Treaty formally commits the United States to provide assistance to any member state that has been the object of a military attack. The

United States has a population, economy and armed force far bigger than that of any European country. However, because the United States is a hegemon, European governments have much less voice in its policies than in the Council of the European Union. Moreover, decision-making about security is now subject to a polarised American political system and President Donald Trump has declared that European governments must spend more to defend themselves if they want to rely on America's protection.

Climate change is a global problem because pollution crosses continents and more pollution is created in Asia and North America than in Europe. The United Nations' inclusive membership gives it a global reach and it has taken the lead in recommending policies that member governments ought to adopt to protect the climate. However, the UN lacks the power to enforce its recommendations and its biggest polluters, such as China, the United States and India, can ignore its proposals.

In a democracy public opinion matters and voters can be sceptical of alliances that dilute the electoral accountability of decision-makers. Governments must educate their citizens about gains in effectiveness that alliances can bring or risk voters rejecting an alliance, as happened in the United Kingdom with Brexit. There are many theories about why people want their country to go it alone when their security is at risk, as Chapter 3 explains. One is that people are democratic nationalists; they do not want to share their influence on the government with foreign institutions. Another theory is that those who reject alliances are uneducated and distrust foreigners, people whom Hillary Clinton referred to as 'deplorables'.

Our model of how Europeans view a threatening world poses two questions: Do individuals see their country facing big security threats? If so, do they want their government to respond on its own or turn for help to alliances? Public opinion surveys provide appropriate evidence to answer these questions. In this book we analyse original data from the European Security Survey (EuroSec). It interviewed 12,685 people in eight countries—the United Kingdom, Germany, Poland, Sweden, Romania, Hungary, Italy and Croatia. All but the United Kingdom belong to three major security alliances, the European Union, NATO and the United Nations. Interviewing occurred almost a year after Russia invaded Ukraine.

Security threats are not facts: they are subjective political judgments that individuals construct in their minds. While government ministers responsible for national security cannot ignore risks to national security, ordinary Europeans may do so until they materialise in their own lives through inflation, abnormal weather or bombs dropped by drones. Hence, the first step in the EuroSec survey is to ask whether people think their country faces a fair or big risk from potential security threats. Chapter 4 analyses the replies. Most people see at least a fair risk, but the proportion doing so varies greatly between military, economic and climate threats.

Faced with a variety of threats, governments have a choice of joining an alliance or dealing with the threat on their own. The survey offers respondents who see a significant risk five alternatives: getting help from the European Union, the United Nations, NATO or the United States, or their national government looking after a risk on its own. Chapter 5 reports the extent to which concerned Europeans want their country to work with allies; the size of the majority varies substantially between security threats. Going it alone enables voters to influence directly what governors do. A plurality but less than a majority of Europeans think their country is better-off defending itself on its own from the global economy and climate change. There is, however, an awareness that in military matters their national resources are dwarfed by the United States and Russia; less than one-quarter want their country to go it alone in military defence.

Multi-national alliances offer a country the chance to increase the effectiveness of its security by pooling resources with other countries. European citizens make discriminating judgments about the EU's capacity to provide security. Their opinion of the EU varies according to the type of threat and the EU's resources. Its substantial economic powers are reflected in it being by far the most desirable ally for dealing with the global economy. When the focus is on climate change, the choice of ally is divided. Almost one-third endorse the EU while one-quarter favour allying with the United Nations.

When help is needed to deal with military aggression, Europeans have turned their backs on Brussels and looked across the Atlantic. NATO, which is dominated by the United States, is seen as the best source of military help by a majority of respondents. An additional 9 per cent explicitly choose protection by the United States. However, only two per cent see the United States as a major ally in dealing with climate change and four per cent as an ally in dealing with the global economy. Moreover, President Trump's electoral success cautions against over-reliance on the United States.

Although all European countries are long-standing members of the United Nations, Europeans recognise that the global inclusiveness of its membership limits what it can do to promote security. Security Council measures supported by Britain and France can be vetoed by Russia or China. When the UN does despatch peace-keeping forces, they go to places beyond Europe. Thus, few Europeans see the UN as helpful in dealing with their own military or economic security. There is, however, a significant minority that think the UN could help protect against climate change, an intercontinental problem.

While a national government speaks with one voice, their citizens are divided about whether the government should act within an alliance or go it alone. This is not because people see alliances as over-riding the democratic accountability of their governors. The statistical analyses in Chapter 5 show that people who place more value on living in a democracy are also more likely to favour working with allies. It is because a substantial proportion of Europeans want to protect their national economy from foreign trade and their national sovereignty from being infringed upon; this makes them tend to favour their country going it alone on specific security issues.

A majority of Europeans are pragmatic; their choice of allies varies with the problem at hand. They reject the ambition of European federalists to create a European Union that protects all forms of security. Instead, they favour differentiated integration, switching between the EU, NATO, the UN or their own national government for their security rather than putting all hopes in one institution. Chapter 6 explains this as due to Europeans wanting their security to be functionally effective, and the effectiveness of multi-national alliances varies from one type of problem to another.

Since the European Security Survey can only reflect the state of public opinion at a single point in time, our study concludes by marshalling evidence of the extent to which public opinion about security issues changes. In response to the ups and downs of the global economy since the 2008 global recession, there has been a tendency for the percentage favouring the EU as an ally to increase. By contrast, the very high percentage of Europeans favouring the trans-Atlantic NATO alliance has remained high in Europe while it has fallen in the United States. There is a steady public awareness of the seriousness of the risk of climate change and a growing readiness to turn to the EU for help.

Implications

The definition of security problems reflects different social science approaches. This book adds to the understanding of European security by integrating multiple social science approaches to analyse an essential public policy, the protection of national security. Since European institutions do not authorise an armed force, studies of European integration have concentrated on how politics has broadened the EU's economic policies and the Maastricht Treaty adding to the European Union a new High Representative for Foreign Affairs and Security Policy. This has stimulated a growing literature about what the EU does in foreign affairs in different continents and, since the Russian invasion of Ukraine, what it is doing to co-ordinate actions by a number of member states to support Ukraine. This book takes the measure of the EU's security policy by making comparisons between public support for the EU as a security ally as against NATO.

Within the field of international relations, power politics provided the theoretical base for security studies concentrating on the role of force during the cold war. This book focuses on a fresh issue raised by President Donald Trump: How willing are Europeans to provide for their military defence, collectively or by each country going it alone? The focus on security in the global economy and in a world with a changing climate is in keeping with the broadening of security studies to examine many different types of security threats beyond those posed by military force.

The European Security Survey is a study in the comparative politics of public opinion. It compares evidence of how people see three different types of security and five different choices of alliances and it tests whether people differ in their views because they live in eight different national contexts. Insofar as countries share common goals and agreement on means, popular support for a multi-national alliance is reasonable. The EU and NATO periodically commission public opinion surveys asking questions about threats to security and support for themselves. Our approach adds value because it shows how each alliance competes with other alliances in offering help to defend a particular form of security. It also offers respondents the option of rejecting multi-national alliances and endorsing going it alone to protect their security.

Since a broad range of readers from students to policymakers are interested in national security, we present our analysis in clear language free of technical jargon and copious citations more appropriate to a PhD thesis. Additional technical details are available online through links given in the text. The European Security Survey data set is available as one module of an omnibus survey that can be accessed at https://www.scripts-berlin.eu/research/research-projects/Short-term-Projects/2022_FIFA_Qatar/index.html for further analysis by students and lecturers.

In writing this book we have benefitted from the support of the Wissenschaftszentrum Berlin für Sozialforschung, where Bernhard Weßels analyses European public opinion and Richard Rose is a visiting fellow. The European Security Survey is part of the research project Public Attitudes towards the Liberal Script (PALS) supported by the German Science Foundation. Full information about the survey and the data file are available at https://www.scripts-berlin.eu/research/pals/data-and-documentation/index.html

February 2025

Bernhard Weßels
Richard Rose

About This Book

The governments of Europe today face major threats to national security from the global economy, military action and climate change. This book shows the extent to which ordinary European citizens likewise see big threats to their security. Insofar as this is the case, do they think the European Union or other institutions–NATO, the United States or the UN–is best placed to help them? Or do people think that their security is better protected if their government goes it alone? These questions are answered by analysing the evidence in the European Security Survey, which interviewed 12,685 people in eight European countries after Russia's invasion of Ukraine. It shows under what circumstances the European Union is seen as the best ally for security and when it is not. The survey also identifies the political attitudes and socio-economic characteristics that influence individuals to turn to allies for help or rely just on their national government for security.

Contents

1	**How Threats to Security Differ**	1
	1.1 Threats Have Different Histories	3
	1.2 Threats Vary in Their Impact	7
	1.3 Managing Security	10
	References	13
2	**A Choice of Allies**	15
	2.1 Resources for Going It Alone	17
	2.2 A Choice of Multi-national Alliances	20
	References	27
3	**Public Opinion Matters**	29
	3.1 How Security Matters at the Grassroots	32
	3.2 A Model of Individual Security Choices	36
	3.3 The European Security Survey	39
	References	41
4	**Sizing Up Threats**	43
	4.1 Perceptions of Global Threats	44
	4.2 Who Sees Their Security Threatened?	46
	References	54

5	**Who Wants Which Allies?**	55
	5.1 Going It Alone	57
	5.2 Diversified Support for Diverse Allies	62
	References	72
6	**Europeans Pragmatic About Security**	73
	6.1 Security Is About Effectiveness	75
	6.2 Pressures to Change	79
	References	86

Appendix: List of Variables   87

List of Figures

Fig. 3.1	A model of individual perceptions of threats	37
Fig. 3.2	A model of choice or rejection of an alliance	38
Fig. 5.1	Support for going it alone in security	59
Fig. 6.1	Trend endorsement of EU as economic ally	80
Fig. 6.2	Trend endorsement of EU helping with climate change	81

List of Tables

Table 3.1	European countries differ in resources	41
Table 4.1	How Europeans see risks to national security	45
Table 4.2	Influences on perception of risks	49
Table 5.1	Influences on going it alone in national security	60
Table 5.2	Choice of ally differs by security threat	63
Table 5.3	Influences on wanting EU as economic ally	66
Table 5.4	Influences on wanting UN or EU as climate change ally	68
Table 5.5	Influences on wanting a military ally	69

CHAPTER 1

How Threats to Security Differ

Abstract We live in a time of polycrisis, when governments all over Europe face multiple and serious security threats that differ in form. Military action involves the confrontation of armed forces; the global economy requires the movement of money and trade across borders; and climate is changing due to heat-inducing substances injected into the atmosphere. These threats affect many levels of society from the individual household worried about inflation to global policymakers grappling with climate change. Threats to national security can come from other states; non-state organisations; trans-national processes such as international markets; or natural phenomena. To understand how collective security threats differ, this chapter contrasts differences in their histories that remain significant today. It examines how security threats differ in their causes and in how they impact society. To protect against threats, prime ministers must rely on inputs from a variety of institutions when making decisions about security. Decisions are often the outcome of conflicts between the multiple institutions concerned with security.

Keywords Threats · Security · War · Global economy · Climate · Defence · European Union · NATO · UN

© The Author(s), under exclusive license to Springer Nature Switzerland AG 2025
B. Weßels and R. Rose, *European Public Opinion about Security*, Palgrave Studies in European Union Politics,
https://doi.org/10.1007/978-3-031-86263-2_1

Governments all over Europe face multiple and serious security threats that differ in form. Military action involves the confrontation of armed forces; the global economy requires the movement of money and trade across borders; and the climate is changing due to heat-inducing substances injected into the earth's atmosphere. These threats affect many levels of society from the individual household worried about inflation to global policymakers grappling with climate change (cf. Baele and Jalea 2023).

Initially security studies concentrated on national governments using military threats to impose their will on less powerful states (Buzan and Hansen 2009). By contrast, the United Nations Development Programme defines human security in people-centred terms, focusing on the welfare of individuals in developing societies, who lack basic resources to maintain a desirable way of life (cf. UNDP 1994; Martin and Owen 2013). Studies of globalisation often deal with threats arising from the activities of global elites and multi-national corporations (Roberts and Lamp 2021).

Threats to national security can come from other states; non-state organisations; trans-national processes such as international markets; or natural phenomena. This results in big differences in how a government can respond to a threat. Military threats are the clearest, since they come from a foreign state that a government can confront with force, negotiate with or be forced to surrender to. Multi-national enterprises operating in international markets may be affected by the strategic decisions of a few governments, but most governments are decision-takers rather than decision-makers in the global economy.

The threat of global climate change comes from an accumulation of human activities beyond the reach of a single government.

The impact of security threats differs too. Military defeat can cause the loss of a country's freedom and territory. The global economy can have a national impact when inflation affects all consumers or a foreign state weaponises its control of a valuable resource to influence another state, as Russia has done with energy. Climate change threatens the way of life and even the survival of the whole of a country's population.

Threats to security from military action, global economic recession and climate change are collective because they can have a pervasive effect on the whole of a society's population. By contrast, many threats to security directly impact a portion of society such as individuals in poverty or a minority ethnic group. Because the threats are collective, people cannot achieve security through their own actions. Individuals must rely on their national government to do what it can and, if it deems it appropriate, to enhance its effectiveness by joining an alliance.

To understand how collective security threats differ, the next section contrasts differences in their histories that remain significant today. The following section examines how security threats differ in their causes and in how they impact society. To protect against threats, national governments depend on a variety of institutions on which a prime minister must rely when making decisions about security. The management of national security is in the hands of an ecology of institutions that create major differences within a national government. Decisions are often the outcome of conflicts between the multiple institutions concerned with security.

1.1 Threats Have Different Histories

Threats from military action, the global economy and climate change have risen and fallen independently of each other in keeping with their different causes. By contrast to today's polycrisis, there have been times when there was no major threat to security from any of these sources (see Rose 2025).

Military Insecurity and Security. The end of the Second World War in 1945 was meant to lead to peace as the result of the defeat of Germany, which had launched two major European wars in 25 years. The chief victorious powers—the United States, the Soviet Union and the United Kingdom—met at Potsdam near Berlin to agree to the terms on which security could be jointly maintained. However, military insecurity followed.

Countries liberated from German occupation expected to be self-governing and have the right to make their own foreign and defence policies. However, Joseph Stalin believed the Soviet Union's military security would be best maintained by building a buffer zone against another German invasion by stationing troops across Eastern and much of Central Europe. Unfree elections placed national governments in the hands of communist parties loyal to Moscow. The Warsaw Pact confirmed Soviet command of a military alliance of eight countries with a combined population of more than 250 million people. The Soviet blockade of Berlin in 1948–1949 raised military insecurity to a peak.

The creation of the North Atlantic Treaty Organization (NATO) in 1949 stabilised military security in a cold war that lasted for four decades.

It did so by creating a 12-country military alliance for collective defence. Since NATO included the United States, a nuclear superpower, this was sufficient to deter Soviet forces from breaching the Iron Curtain that divided Europe. NATO's commitment to deterrence rather than expansion eastwards was shown in 1956, when it did not send troops to the aid of Hungary when Soviet troops crushed that country's attempt to break free of Moscow's domination.

The collapse of the Soviet military bloc and the introduction of free elections in Eastern Europe after the fall of the Berlin Wall in 1989 was hailed as the end of a history of European wars, since democracies do not make war against each other. The break-up of the Soviet Union at the end of 1991 created a weak Russian Federation and led West European governments to enjoy a fiscal dividend from peace. Reduced military expenditure made available more money to spend on popular domestic social services. Eleven ex-communist states joined NATO to gain greater protection against a recurrence of Russian aggression.

President Vladimir Putin has shown that Europe's history of military insecurity was suspended, not ended. In keeping with his view that the collapse of the Soviet Union was 'the greatest geopolitical catastrophe of the century', Putin has sought to restore Moscow's dominance by military means. In 2008 Russian troops carved out of the country of Georgia an area that the Russian Federation then annexed. In 2014 troops wearing uniforms without national insignia seized power in Crimea and parts of eastern Ukraine, both areas with predominantly ethnically Russian populations. The territories were then formally incorporated in the Russian Federation. European countries reacted against Russia's use of force with diplomatic protests rather than force.

Russia's military invasion of Ukraine in 2022 has made dealing with military insecurity a high-level concern of governments in Europe, as many NATO states border either Russia, its satellite Belarus or Ukraine. Finland and Sweden have abandoned neutrality and joined NATO. National governments and the European Union have given economic aid and military equipment to support Ukraine fighting a proxy war for the defence of Europe (IfW Kiel 2024). President Donald Trump has added to insecurity by stating that the United States should not come to the defence of European countries that have been free-riding on the American taxpayer by not meeting their NATO spending commitments. European governments have responded by announcing plans to increase defence spending but in doing so have faced fiscal constraints on spending and shortages of military equipment that they can buy.

Economic Security and Globalisation. Historically, major European governments have guarded their economic security by placing barriers such as tariffs on foreign imports. The destruction of national economies caused by the Second World War faced governments with the common challenge of reconstruction to restore their economies. The United States stimulated European co-operation through the Marshall Plan. It offered billions of dollars plus technical assistance on the condition that European governments would agree on how the aid should be shared between them. By the 1950s European countries had recovered from wartime damage sufficiently to provide rising incomes and welfare state policies. This was followed by a sustained period of economic growth.

The European Coal and Steel Community was launched in 1951 to promote economic and military security by integrating major industries of Germany and France that were needed for economic growth and manufacturing military weapons. By 1957 it had evolved into the European Economic Community (EEC), which gradually gained sufficient power to promote economic growth through a Single European Market and monetary stability through the European Central Bank and a common currency, the euro. The EEC founders' effort to provide military security through a European Defence Community failed. The result has been national reliance on different institutions to maintain Europe's economic and military security: the European Union based in Brussels and NATO, led by the president of the United States.

The period of 30 years of outstanding growth that underpinned economic security was abruptly reversed in 1975 by a global recession in which European economies contracted and both inflation and unemployment rose. Invoking loose analogies with Weimar Germany, the unexpected rise in economic insecurity led to fears of the breakdown of democratic governments. The fears were unfounded. The challenge demonstrated the resilience of European institutions. Growth returned and inflation fell as governments turned from Keynesian policies stimulating demand to monetary policies combating inflation (cf. Rose and Peters 1978).

The economic security of Europeans has increasingly been influenced through the EU's integration of trade within a Single European Market and trade in the global economy. This has led to growth in European exports to the United States and China. However, economic crises elsewhere created recession in Europe following the collapse of financial institutions in New York in 2008. The European response demonstrated political resilience (Hellwig et al. 2020). Germany saw increasing trade with Russia as a means of increasing military security by making Russia rely on energy exports for income in euros. The Russian weaponisation of energy exports after its invasion of Ukraine created a turning point. Germany is now seeking energy from politically secure sources. The American identification of the People's Republic of China as a security threat is putting pressure on European countries to reduce trade with China, and the re-election of Donald Trump as president has opened the prospect of a tariff war in the global economy.

A Deteriorating Climate. Since the Ice Age millions of years ago, the earth's climate has been alternating between cooler glacial periods and periods with warm temperatures. The latter prevailed at the start of the Industrial Revolution three centuries ago. Because industry, transportation and agriculture have increased pollution as a by-product of increasing prosperity, this has very slowly but progressively altered the globe's climate by increasing greenhouse gases.

Up to a point, greenhouse gases have had the positive effect of trapping some of the sun's radiation after it reaches the earth and retaining it in the earth's atmosphere. Without greenhouse gases having made the earth warmer, the global temperature would be an estimated 30 °C colder (IPCC 2023). Cumulatively, economic and population growth has enhanced the greenhouse effect, slowly raising the earth's temperature. The estimated temperature in Europe has risen by more than 2 °C since 1850, more than double the global average. Moreover, the temperature is continuing to rise at a rate that will widen the gap between Europe's climate and expert standards for protecting Europe's environment (European Environmental Agency 2023).

Political activists began demonstrating in the 1960s against activities that could potentially change the environment for the worse. In 1971 Greenpeace was founded to carry out non-violent resistance to activities creating climate change and to nuclear developments. It now has national branches lobbying against climate change in Europe and internationally. Its claims of threats to the environment and actions by activists have been criticised on scientific and normative grounds (Wikipedia 2024).

The combination of expert opinion and pressure from political activists led the United Nations to shift from its initial concern with the use of natural resources in economic development to a focus on the conservation of resources. A UN conference on the human environment held in Stockholm in 1972 was dubbed the First Earth Summit. It warned of the potential threat of climate change and recommended further UN action. This led to the establishment of UN bodies to monitor global climate change and recommend actions to reduce threats (Jackson 2007). Since then, 29 UN Climate Change Conferences have made recommendations for protecting the climate.

The great majority of national governments have announced strategies to reduce climate change in future, and the European Union has used its regulatory powers to reduce climate change. This has achieved a major reduction in greenhouse gases and set the goal of Europe achieving neutrality in emissions by 2050. To reach this goal the EU has allocated €578 billion in its 2021–2027 budget.

National governments are promoting positive measures to increase reliance on natural resources such as wind power, tidal power and solar energy and negative controls to reduce heating homes and powering automobiles with fossil fuels. Enterprises have pledged co-operation up to a point, especially when public subsidies are offered to neutralise investment costs and yield a profit. Households have co-operated to some extent, for example installing solar panels to reduce heating costs. However, when changes involve increasing the cost of heating or motoring, Europeans have flinched, and democratic governments have responded by reducing the compulsion for individuals to spend money to reduce domestic emissions.

1.2 Threats Vary in Their Impact

In order to compare threats to national security, we need to identify the different elements that combine to give military action, the global economy and climate change their different characters.

Actors and Causes. In social science terminology, actors can refer to institutions and processes as well as individual politicians. The political leaders of a state are the prime actors making decisions that trigger military action, such as President Putin ordering Russian troops to invade Ukraine in 2022. The long-term causes of Vladimir Putin's decisions reach back to the period when Ukraine was integrated in the Soviet Union and then became independent when the Soviet Union collapsed at the end of 1991. Wars can be caused by competition for land, national recognition or economic resources, leading to a military build-up. Paradoxically, military threats may also be a cause of an absence of action. The logic of deterrence was important in the Cold War, when the United States and Soviet possession of nuclear weapons deterred each side from launching a nuclear attack, as a counter-attack would lead to mutually assured destruction.

The chief actors in the global economy are multi-national companies and financial institutions operating across continents and governments large enough to influence the world's major markets. They are not engaged in zero-sum conflict. They are enterprises engaged in market transactions from which both buyers and sellers may profit. The extent of economic security or insecurity among Europeans is not the result of decisions taken by the European Union and its member states. It is the unplanned by-product of the around-the-clock interaction of markets that connect Europe, North America and Asia (see Lindblom 1965).

Climate change is caused by a great variety of actors releasing what adds up to an excess of greenhouse gases. Manufacturers release dioxides into the atmosphere as a by-product of their factories producing goods. Farmers fertilise crops and raise animals in order to feed an urban population; a by-product of this is a negative effect on the climate. Individuals drive their automobile or take planes to get places that would be difficult or impossible to reach on foot or by bicycle. The Intergovernmental Panel on Climate Change (IPCC 2023: 4) baldly states, 'Human activities, principally through emissions of greenhouse gases, have unequivocally caused global warming'. Thus, almost all of Europe's population is contributing to climate change.

Incidence of Insecurity. A threat to national security can be latent, intermittent or continuously significant. Governments are continuously responsible for security, but the likelihood of a threat to security fluctuates between low and high. Major European countries have not been involved in a war with each other in the lifetime of the great majority of the continent's population. However, since the end of the Second World War there have been times when there was a high threat of military action. It was high in the first few years after 1945 as the Soviet Union used its troops to expand its control of governments as far west as East Berlin and Prague. For a few weeks in 1962 the Cuban missile crisis threatened a nuclear war until negotiations between President John F. Kennedy and Nikita Khrushchev brought about a reversion to a cold peace. The collapse of the Soviet Union in 1991 reduced the likelihood of military conflict for three decades before the Russian invasion of Ukraine in 2022 turned a potential threat into a fact.

By contrast, the global economy is continuously fluctuating, as goods, services and money change hands around the clock around the world. National and European institutions issue monthly, quarterly and annual reports and forecasts of economic growth, inflation and unemployment. Changes in the annual level of prices, employment or economic growth can stimulate a temporary sense of insecurity if they are negative. Over the years there tends to be a cycle in which a national economy rotates between periods of substantial economic growth, a slow pace of growth and occasional recessions, defined as at least six months in which a country's gross domestic product contracts. Over decades European economies have tended to grow substantially notwithstanding short periods of recession (OECD 2019: 75).

The heat, humidity and wind that constitute weather conditions fluctuate within a more or less predictable range every 24 hours, and between seasons. A drought or a tornado is an abnormal interruption of long periods when discussions of the day's weather were not linked to threats to security. However, scientific evidence of long-term climate change shows a cumulative increase in the emission of gases causing a rise in temperature and, given the persistence of this trend, a threat to the climate security of Europeans later in this century.

Impact. When a country is at war, all citizens feel the impact, but the extent of the impact varies. It is strongest in regions where there is ground fighting or aerial bombardment. Those of an age subject to military service can have their lives disrupted and put at risk, and their families suffer anxiety or worse. The impact of defeat can be a state losing a substantial amount of territory and its system of government being replaced by a regime more agreeable to the victor. Winners and losers both face substantial costs of reconstructing a peacetime society and economy. The experience of war can have a long-term impact on public policy. For example, it gave a major impetus to European integration after 1945, and the war in Ukraine has created a sense of military insecurity in European governments.

The frequency of fluctuations in the economy is not matched by their impact on public opinion. Most changes are small. Daily fluctuations in currency values tend to be limited to a fraction of a cent, and monthly fluctuations in inflation and unemployment are often less than a single percentage point. When economic conditions turn negative, the impact is limited for about half the population. Retired people do not have a job to lose, and youths in school have an incentive to study longer and harder. When pensions are inflation-indexed, retired people have their income protected. Changes that have a big impact on people, such as becoming unemployed, directly affect a small proportion of a country's population, and most unemployed people return to work within a matter of months. The impact of the global economy on Europeans is affected by the extent to which it is involved in international trade. Exports are equivalent to about half of Germany's GDP compared to one-third of Britain's and one-quarter of the GDP of the United States. This has meant that Germany has benefited specially from the growth in world trade. It is also specially vulnerable to the threat by the Trump administration to impose tariffs on European countries.

Of the threats discussed here, climate change has potentially the widest and most intense impact. Because climate change is a global phenomenon, it threatens people on every continent, not just Europeans with droughts reducing the supply of food and an increase in floods. Within a country, climate change may affect the whole population or may be concentrated in dense urban populations or coastal areas.

1.3 Managing Security

Threats to security are not problems to be solved; they are problems that must be managed by governments, markets and citizens. Even if a threat is low, a national government must still monitor conditions and be prepared to respond promptly and effectively as and when the threat to security becomes high. Preparations can be made to act alone or through an established alliance membership.

Individual citizens can do little to affect climate change on their own. Even if a person relies more on a bicycle than an automobile or turns down their house temperature a few degrees, such individual actions have an impact only if they are followed by the mass of the population. The stimulus for mass action to protect the climate has come from activists and experts placing the environment on the political agenda. From 2000 to 2023 a total of 31 green parties have contested and won seats in the parliaments of European democracies, and 13 have gained a place in government. Their success has led to parties of other ideologies putting in their election manifestos pro-environment policies such as making a target of net zero or balancing greenhouse gas emissions with greenhouse gas capture by 2050.

The increased awareness of climate security has also created a democratic backlash by revealing the cost of adopting effective policies to reduce threats. As a result, elected politicians have been readier to make verbal commitments to increase national security than to implement measures that would impose substantial costs on voters. For example, in opposition the British Labour Party pledged to spend £28bn a year to promote green policies financed primarily by borrowing. In the run-up to the 2024 British general election, the commitment was abandoned for fear the cost would undermine the party's pledge not to raise taxes once in government. To become a partner in a three-party coalition government in 2021 the German Green Party accepted a delay until 2045 in making the country climate-neutral and abandoned its policy of imposing a speed limit on motorways.

National governments. To manage national security, each European government has a variety of departments concerned dealing with military threats, finance, the management of the economy, environment, energy, agriculture and transport. Departments that are not principally responsible for a security issue high on the political agenda can engage in conceptual stretching, that is, highlighting their security implications in order to gain attention and more money. A department responsible for business can seek subsidies to develop domestic manufactures to replace Chinese imports said to threaten military security. By contrast, a department may engage in conceptual shrinkage, as Germany has done, claiming that profitable trade with Russia and with China does not pose a threat to national security.

The task of managing security is made easy when there is little or no threat to a specific form of security. When there are benefits from an expanding global economy, politicians in control of government are ready to claim credit even if their policies have contributed little to the resulting prosperity. When other European countries appear friendly rather than showing signs of aggression, governors can collect the fiscal dividend of peace by reducing military expenditure and spending the savings on social policies or financing tax cuts. A favourable climate helps crops and flowers bloom, and politicians bask in the sunshine.

When a threat to security becomes significant, responsible departments must co-ordinate their policies. In the face of a military threat, a country's diplomats can engage with the country posing the threat in hopes of avoiding fighting, while its defence department makes a show of military readiness with the equipment it has at hand. If fighting breaks out, armed forces dominate action, and departments such as health and industry become involved in the war effort too.

The many government departments that deal with the economy are divided between those seeking to promote economic growth through trade, increased productivity and innovation; those spending money on social policies such as education and health, which can be described as an investment in a country's human capital; and a ministry of finance that has the task of balancing public expenditure assisting economic growth and social policies with public revenue from taxation. When the global economy is boosting national growth too, striking a fiscal balance is eased.

When changes in the global economy depress a country's economic growth, managing the competition between departments for limited funds requires setting priorities that produce losers as well as winners. Social spending is difficult to squeeze, because of the statutory entitlement of citizens to pensions, health care and education. Commitments to economic spending can be controlled up to a point by delaying infrastructure projects intended to promote economic growth. As long as a clear threat of war is not perceived, then military spending is easier to squeeze, as governments in NATO did when the collapse of the Soviet Union immediately disrupted the military force of Moscow. However, once military action starts, then a government tries to mobilise all the money needed to support its armed forces by raising taxes, becoming heavily indebted through borrowing, and securing foreign aid, as Ukraine is doing today.

Some government departments contribute negatively to climate change. The department of transportation builds and maintains roads and airports that generate pollution; the department of energy is concerned with the supply of fossil fuels for homes and businesses; and commerce departments represent the interest of businesses more concerned with keeping the cost of energy from rising than with decreasing greenhouse gases. Similarly, the armed forces give priority to the effectiveness of military equipment rather than the effect of military aircraft and tanks on the environment.

European governments have substantial powers that can be used to reduce the deterioration of the national climate if the political will is there. Legislation can reduce or ban the emission of pollutants into the atmosphere. High taxes can be imposed on pollutants to reduce their consumption, most visibly on petrol. Positive measures may promote energy-efficient public transport and boost the demand for electric automobiles. Cash and tax subsidies can be given to private enterprises to create energy from renewable resources such as wind and ocean tides.

Identifying a security problem is no assurance that a national government can find a solution. First of all, it may lack the resources for effective action. This is most evident in military terms: Russia has a population that is more than twelve times that of the median European country. Moreover, it has a government that has shown the will to use military force. While the income of the average European is well above the global average, the total GDP of the average European country is a small fraction of the national GDP of China. These differences mean that even if a European country does achieve net zero in combating climate change, the effect on global climate change will be small by comparison with the world's populous polluters. Since most European countries face threats to security that exceed their resources to meet, this is an incentive for a national government to boost its security by joining a multi-national alliance.

References

Baele, Stephane and Jalea, Diana, 2023. 'Twenty-Five Years of Securitization Theory: A Corpus-Based Review', *Political Studies Review*, 21, 2, 376–389.

Buzan, Barry and Hansen, Lene, 2009. *The Evolution of International Security Studies*. Cambridge: Cambridge University Press.

European Environmental Agency, 2023. *Global and European Temperatures: Analysis and Data; Indicators*. Copenhagen: www.eea.europa.eu.

Hellwig, Timothy, Kweon, Yesola and Vowles, Jack, 2020. *Democracy under Siege: Parties, Voters and Elections after the Great Recession*. New York: Oxford University Press.

IfW Kiel (Institut für Weltwirtschaft), 2024. *Ukraine Support Tracker*. https://www.ifw-kiel.de/topics/war-against-ukraine/ukraine-support-tracker/.

IPCC (Intergovernmental Panel on Climate Change), 2023. *Climate Change: Synthesis Report Summary for Policymakers*. Geneva: Intergovernmental Panel on Climate Change, https://doi.org/10.59327/IPCC/AR6-9789291691647.001.

Jackson, Peter, 2007. 'From Stockholm to Kyoto: A Brief History of Climate Change', *Green Our World*, 44, 2.

Lindblom, Charles E., 1965. *The Intelligence of Democracy*. New York: Free Press.

Martin, Mary and Owen, Taylor, eds., 2013. *Routledge Handbook of Human Security*. London: Routledge.

OECD (Organisation for Economic Co-operation and Development), 2019. *Society Indicators*. Paris: OECD.

Roberts, Anthea and Lamp, Nicolas, 2021. *Six Faces of Globalization: Who Wins, Who Loses, and Why It Matters*. Cambridge, MA: Harvard University Press.

Rose, Richard, 2025. *European Security from Ukraine to Washington*. London: Bloomsbury Academic.

Rose, Richard and Peters, B. Guy, 1978. *Can Government Go Bankrupt?* New York: Basic Books.

UNDP (United Nations Development Programme), 1994. *Human Development Report 1994*. Oxford: Oxford University Press.

Wikipedia, 2024. 'Criticisms of Greenpeace', https://en.wikipedia.org/wikiCriticismof_Greenpeace.

CHAPTER 2

A Choice of Allies

Abstract When confronted with a threat to security, a European government can respond on its own or join an alliance. Because a democratic government is accountable to its electorate for security, it may choose to act on its own to avoid diluting its power to act. However, in order to act effectively, a government needs substantial resources, and joining a multinational alliance can enhance national resources. There are hundreds of institutions that a government can ally with to increase its resources; these differ in their powers and specialised purposes. The European Union is a multi-purpose alliance with strong powers to deal with economic security; significant powers to deal with climate change; and very little authority to deal with military defence. The United Nations Charter lists a variety of purposes. However, the very inclusiveness of its membership greatly limits its effectiveness, since the governments threatening security are member states as are states wanting protection. The North Atlantic Treaty Organization by contrast is an alliance with a clear purpose: to protect its member states against military attack. The great majority of European states belong to alliances to help deal with threats to their security and engage in political bargaining with other governments that restrict their independence.

Keywords Resources · Threats · Security · Population · War · Moscow · GDP · European Union · NATO · UN

© The Author(s), under exclusive license to Springer Nature Switzerland AG 2025
B. Weßels and R. Rose, *European Public Opinion about Security*, Palgrave Studies in European Union Politics,
https://doi.org/10.1007/978-3-031-86263-2_2

National independence and interdependence are opposite sides of the coin that European governments rely on to maintain national security. When confronted with a threat to security, a European government can respond on its own or join an alliance. Because a democratic government is accountable to its electorate for security, it may choose to act on its own to avoid diluting its power to act. However, in order to act effectively, a government needs substantial resources, and joining a multi-national alliance offers a major means to enhance national resources.

To deter a military threat, a national government needs a large, well-equipped army. That is why big states tend to threaten small states and states that give a low priority to military defence. To deal with threats from the global economy, a country needs a degree of self-sufficiency in producing food and goods and a positive balance of trade to pay for its imports from foreign countries. A government has the legal authority and resources to regulate the industries and the behaviour of citizens that affect its climate. However, the effect is limited insofar as major threats come from pollutants that move across national and continental boundaries.

There are hundreds of institutions that a government can ally with to increase its resources; they vary in their powers and their specialised purposes. The European Union is a multi-purpose alliance of 27 member states with strong powers to deal with economic security; significant powers to deal with climate change; and very little authority to deal with military defence. The current ambitions of the EU reflect mission creep. It was founded in 1957 to enhance the economies of its member states. Since then it has adopted a range of policies that, as the Treaty of Rome stated, 'lay the foundations of an ever closer union among the peoples of Europe'.

The United Nations Charter lists a variety of purposes: to prevent war, to promote justice and human rights, to advance social progress and freedom and to encourage respect for international law. However, the very inclusiveness of its membership greatly limits its effectiveness, since the governments threatening security are member states as are states wanting protection. While the United Nations has limited authority to put its multiple policy goals into effect, it also has few constraints on what it can address, so it has been able to expand the subjects it monitors and makes advisory statements about.

The North Atlantic Treaty Organization, by contrast, is an alliance with a purpose: to protect its 32 member states against military attack.

NATO is distinctive in having kept to its original narrow purpose: the military defence of its member states against an aggressor in Europe. Most member states have been successful in resisting pressure from Washington to join with the United States in the use of force on other continents.

Alliances differ in the extent to which they reduce accountability. The greater the obligation of a member government to accept collective decisions, the less the influence of the national electorate to which it is democratically accountable. European Union institutions have exclusive powers to act in international trade negotiations, and the monetary policy of many European governments is determined by the European Central Bank, not by national central banks. Article 5 of the NATO Treaty commits member states to come to the defence of any member that is subject to a military attack. The NATO alliance thus obligates the United States to protect the territorial security of countries distant from American borders. The United Nations has the least impact on the accountability of democratic governments to their electorate, since member states can follow or ignore UN recommendations as they choose.

The default position for national governments is to deal with security problems on their own, since a political effort is required to join an alliance and maintain popular support for accepting its obligations. Nonetheless, the great majority of European states prefer to belong to alliances to help deal with threats to their security. The next section identifies resource limitations that discourage countries from defending themselves on their own. It is followed by an analysis of the advantages that a country gains by joining an alliance and the limitations of a country having its security depend on political bargaining among allies rather than on its own national government.

2.1 Resources for Going It Alone

Each European government has the political legitimacy to deal with security threats on its own. However, its capacity to act effectively depends on the resources it can mobilise compared to the resources of its challenger. There are big differences between countries in the size of their resources. There are also significant political differences between countries in their readiness to mobilise resources.

Population. The size of a country's population has a direct effect on multiple security resources. It sets a ceiling on the size of its armed forces. The proportion of the population mobilised for military service varies with a government's perception of military threats and policies about military training. Since the collapse of the Soviet Union, a majority of European countries have relied solely on a volunteer army, and one-third have a form of compulsory military service for at least six months (https://en.wikipedia.org/wiki/List_of_enlistment_age_by_country). In the extreme case of Ukraine, the government has obligated men up to the age of 50 to join its army in resistance to Russian invaders. The increased military expenditure by European countries in response to Russia's invasion of Ukraine has been allocated primarily to buying military hardware rather than to increasing the size of their uniformed forces.

Population also influences the size of a country's national economy. Its gross domestic product reflects the output of its labour force, and population sets a limit on the number of people who can produce its goods and services. The size of its official labour force is modified by laws on compulsory education and the age of retirement as well as by gender differences between men and women. In contemporary Europe men are 10% more likely to be in paid employment than women (Rose 2024: chapter 7).

The population of European countries is extremely skewed: it ranges from 83 million in Germany to just over half a million each in Malta and Luxembourg. Moreover, four countries—Germany, the United Kingdom, France and Italy—collectively have half of Europe's population, while there are eight countries that each have less than 1% of the continent's population. By contrast, the population of Russia, which poses the chief military threat to European countries, is approximately 140 million. Russia's population is more than double the size of every European country except Germany and three and a half times Ukraine (https://ec.europa.eu/eurostat/databrowser/view/tps00001/default/table?lang=en&category=t_demo.t_demo_pop).

Economy. A country with a large GDP will have sufficient money to maintain a well-paid armed force equipped with weapons that it manufactures itself or imports, such as American aircraft. It will also have enough weight to influence as well as be influenced by activities in the global economy. However, insofar as a country's wealth includes a large industrial sector, it will have a substantial number of enterprises polluting the atmosphere.

There are two familiar measures of a country's economy: the size of its total GDP and the average value of an individual's income. For comparative purposes, both can be measured in US dollars and the dollar value adjusted for cross-national differences in purchasing power. There is a great range in the size of the total GDP of European Union countries. Five European countries have a GDP greater than one trillion dollars, while six have a total GDP of less than 100 billion dollars. In the global economy, most European economies appear small. Germany's GDP, currently the fourth-largest in the world, is about to be overtaken by that of India, and it is one-sixth that of the world's leader, the United States.

Differences in the size of national economies tend to reflect differences in national population. There is a correlation of 0.81 between the size of a country's population and its GDP. If the per capita GDP of a country is high, then individual Europeans will be better cushioned to absorb the impact of a global recession on their economic security. However, individual prosperity is not linked to the size of a country's GDP. Ireland and Luxembourg have much higher GDP per capita than Spain and Poland.

Although the total GDP of Russia is less than that of leading European countries, the country has mobilised its resources in a war economy to fight Ukraine. It is estimated to spend more than 7% of its GDP on its military force. Moreover, Russia engages in low-cost cyber-attacks and disinformation campaigns and has used the supply of energy as a weapon in efforts to influence European security.

Geography. A country's geographical location is a significant resource for security from invasion by a neighbouring country. Russia has demonstrated its readiness to use its armed forces to invade neighbouring countries. Eight countries extending from Finland to Romania border Russia, its Belarus satellite or Ukraine. The importance of proximity is augmented by Russia having a population almost four times that of Poland, its most populous neighbour, and one hundred times that of its least populous neighbour, Estonia. Neighbouring governments have responded by spending above-average shares of their GDP on defence and aid to Ukraine.

Countries least accessible to Russia are most secure against invasion by a Russian army. This category is led by eight European countries with a border on the Atlantic Ocean and having at least one country between their own territory and Russia. The countries extend from Ireland and Denmark to Spain and Portugal. The distance of a country's national capital from Moscow is a rough indicator of vulnerability to air attacks. Countries having major natural resources within their territory benefit from the economic advantage this yields. Coal was a major source of energy during the Industrial Revolution, and Bismarck based Germany's security policy on having iron and coal to produce military equipment. This was recognised in 1951 by the creation of the European Coal and Steel Community to place these materials under supra-national control so that Germany would no longer have the resources in its hands that it had previously relied upon to fight and win wars with France.

Energy is a major resource for a country's economy but its use is also a major threat to climate change. The emission of carbon dioxide is the major manmade activity increasing greenhouse gases that threaten the environment. The extent to which national economies are threatening their own economy is indicated by the kilotons of fossil CO_2 emissions they produce each year. As concern about climate change has been increasing, European countries in 2022 produced less CO_2 than previously, while large differences remained between countries.

Germany accounted for nearly one-quarter of all European emissions, more than double those of the United Kingdom, which was second. Whether the measure is military, economic or geography, no European country has enough resources to be confident of defending its security on its own. The population of the median European country is only 7% that of Russia, and the GDP of the median European country is less than one-fifth that of Russia. While a majority of European countries do not have a border facing Russian troops, as Germany found at the end of the Second World War, once East European countries are occupied by an invader, Russian troops are closer to Berlin than to Moscow and also closer to Paris.

2.2 A Choice of Multi-national Alliances

Belonging to a multi-national alliance helps a national government increase its effectiveness, since it can pool the resources of a dozen or more countries to deal with threats to its national security. However, alliances also impose a political cost because decisions are taken collectively; thus, each government is greatly outnumbered by its partners. Collective decision-making can impose a policy that a national government would not take on its own and does not want to be held accountable for by its national electorate.

The incentive for a government to join an alliance is that pooling resources multiplies its capacity to act effectively. The resources of an alliance are usually additive, as in NATO, which has a combined military force that is far larger than that of the median member state or of Russia. Similarly, the Single European Market, given its collective size, greatly expands the trade of each member state. However, it also increases the scope for economic competition. Because of its large and heterogeneous membership, the United Nations is rarely an alliance with a common cause; instead, the resources of member states are withheld from pooling or divided by alliances more effective than the UN.

Alliances differ in many ways. Alliances may be focused on a single purpose such as military security or have multiple and heterogeneous functions such as the United Nations. Secondly, they differ in the extent to which they are supported by treaties and supra-national institutions that have the power to impose obligations on members or regard allies as sovereign states.

The European Union. There were many visions of how European countries could maintain their security after the end of the Second World War. Before the war ended Italian anti-fascists led by Altiero Spinelli proposed a federal Union (cf. Mayne et al. 1990). In a 1946 speech in Zurich, Winston Churchill endorsed a vaguely defined United States of Europe with Britain and its Commonwealth outside it. Charles de Gaulle spoke approvingly of a *Europe des États* or a *Europe des patries*, in which policies were made by intergovernmental negotiations between independent states (Teasdale 2016).

The progenitors of the European Union such as the Frenchman Jean Monnet envisioned European integration advancing through three alliances with complementary functions: the European Economic Community (EEC), the European Defence Community and the European Political Community. However, the French National Assembly rejected the Pleven Plan for a European Defence Community in 1954 because it feared German re-armament. Thus, two of the three proposed alliances were aborted.

The EEC came into being in 1957 with a primary commitment to economic integration. Its founders were also committed to extending its functions to cover ground left open by the absence of the defence and political communities. Over more than half a century, the EEC has adopted treaties that have greatly expanded its economic functions, which were originally limited to the promotion of trade among its six founder members. This has led to the development of a single European market, the European Central Bank replacing national currencies with the euro, and regulations for social protection against market abuses. The EEC's regulatory powers also give it influence on some economic activities that affect the European climate.

The EEC was turned into the European Union by the 1992 Maastricht Treaty, which explicitly broadened engagement with military security. Its preamble expresses the aspiration for the EU to:

> assert its identity on the international scene, in particular through the implementation of a common foreign and security policy including the progressive framing of a common defence policy, which might lead to a common defence.

The means to achieve this goal is described by the vague term 'strategic autonomy' (Keukeleire and Delreux 2022: 75f; Rieker and Giske 2024). It expresses a desire for the EU to have a recognised standing in global affairs, engaging in activities in developing countries and troubled places in the Balkans. On the other hand, it also reflects a French-led initiative to make the EU less dependent on the United States, a concern heightened by Barack Obama's tilt of American foreign policy to the Pacific and reinforced by President Donald Trump forcefully telling European governments to spend more on defence and that they cannot rely on the United States to come to their defence in all circumstances, as they had previously done.

While the EU has primary powers to make economic decisions that take precedence over those of national governments, in foreign affairs and defence its status is secondary to the power of France and the United Kingdom. Each of those countries has nuclear weapons and a permanent seat with a veto in the United Nations Security Council. The European Union has only observer status at the UN and no voting rights. The EU's diplomatic corps, the European External Action Service, represents the EU in more than one hundred countries. However, in each national capital it must compete for attention with embassies of member states giving priority to advancing their national interests (Ewers-Peters 2022). In Washington, for example, national embassies deal directly as appropriate with the Departments of State, Defence and Commerce and with members of Congress and congressional committees as well as with the White House's National Security Council.

The decision-making procedures of the European Union are designed to give the national government of every member state a voice in the bargaining process that arrives at major decisions, especially those involving security. The heads of national governments meet collectively in the European Council, which can set policy guidelines for the European Commission, including its High Representative for Foreign Affairs and Security Policy. On matters of exceptional importance, the unanimous agreement of member states is required. This gives a single state a veto over the grant of additional security powers. Thus, Hungary's Viktor Orban has been able to use his country's veto power to hold up assistance to Ukraine. Most policies, by contrast, require endorsement by a qualified majority consisting of the EU's most populous states and a majority of smaller states.

When bargaining within the EU does not lead to a consensus, differentiated integration can occur, in which some countries adopt a policy while others do not (Leuffen et al. 2012). For example, a big majority of EU states belong to the eurozone, while a few countries such as Denmark have chosen to be outside. Poland is formally expected to join, but has not sought admission or complied with eurozone standards. While the EU coordinates financial assistance to Ukraine, each member state decides on its own whether and how much to contribute.

The collective resources of the EU are large by comparison with each member state, a reason for countries becoming members. However, since security policies depend for effectiveness on interactions with other member states, the important question is how each state's resources compare with those of major powers involved in systems of global interdependence.

In military affairs, the EU collectively has a population three times that of its proximate threat, Russia, and a total GDP more than six times that of Russia. These resources are leveraged by being pooled for military defence with the United States in NATO. While the population of the United States is one-quarter less than that of the EU, its armed forces are incomparably larger because the EU has no army.

The GDP of EU countries in total accounts for about one-sixth of the world's total GDP. It ranks second in size to the United States in nominal terms, but third behind China when GDP is calculated on the basis of purchasing power parity. Notwithstanding a high level of economic activity, EU countries collectively contribute only 7% of the world's total greenhouse gas emissions. Emissions are below those of India, China and the United States. Moreover, the emission of greenhouse gases has been falling faster in Europe than on other continents.

Although the EU's leaders aspire to a global role, this is not the chief motive for many European countries belonging. Membership greatly leverages the resources of most European states and gives each a voice in political and economic discussions with European states with much greater resources than its own. The median member gains the added effectiveness that comes with a collective population that is more than 40 times larger than its own and a collective GDP that is also far greater.

NATO. By contrast with the EU, which has tried to take on more and more functions of a state, the North Atlantic Treaty Organization has remained close to its founding purpose: to deter Russian military aggression against its members. It has done so by maintaining a large nuclear-armed force drawing on much greater resources than Russia has. While NATO's founding treaty assumed that the United States regarded military aggression in Europe as a threat to American security too, the election of Donald Trump as president has questioned this optimistic European assumption.

From its founding in 1949, the number of NATO members has grown from 12 countries to 32, significantly increased its collective resources and broadened its commitment to defend virtually the whole of the European continent. A major motive for European countries joining NATO is that no European country has the resources to deter Russia on its own nor can the EU offer military protection.

The expansion of NATO has not diminished the dominant American contribution to the organisation, because the US population has grown by more than 180 million people since 1950. It contributes half of NATO's total of 3.5 million active armed forces and more than six times that of any European state. The effectiveness of American forces is enhanced by the sheer amount of its military equipment. This is due to spending a substantially higher proportion of a massive GDP on defence than almost any other NATO member. In 2023 the United States spent $916bn on military defence, two-fifths of the global total of military expenditure.

Distance from Europe protects the United States from the land-based invasion that threatens most European countries, and its repertoire of nuclear weapons and long-range missile systems is a deterrent to a Russian missile attack. American military resources are much greater than those of Russia, albeit they are more widely spread around the world, a reflection of the priority Washington gives to maintaining its security in the Pacific as well as in Europe.

Formally, the North Atlantic Council is the highest decision-making body in NATO; its membership consists of senior civilian representatives of each member state. It is complemented by a complex military structure in which leading positions are held by high-ranking European and American military officers. The Supreme Allied Command Europe (SACEUR) is in command of military operations; the post is held by an American officer, starting with General Dwight D. Eisenhower. This arrangement does not derogate from American military forces remaining under the control of the United States president as their commander-in-chief.

Given its resources, the United States is the de facto hegemon in NATO. Article 5 of NATO's Treaty delegates to national governments the power to decide what action each country takes in response to an attack on another NATO member. This condition was included in order to ensure that the treaty would not be rejected by the United States Congress, which was and remains unready to transfer its constitutional right to declare war to a multi-national institution. The White House retains the power to decide whether an attack on a particular European country is met by an American military response. President Donald Trump's expressions of doubt about whether it is in the American national interest to defend every European country has unsettled Europe's long-standing confidence that the United States would defend its security (see Chapter 6).

United Nations. The founding charter of the United Nations proclaims not only a desire to promote the basic security concerns of peace and prosperity but also defines a multiplicity of functions well beyond these fundamental responsibilities of government. The UN's global orientation gives it 193 member states, more than six times the membership of the European Union or of NATO. Its 15-member Security Council has only two permanent European members, France and the United Kingdom; three other European countries, Malta, Slovenia and Switzerland, were among the Council's rotating members in 2024. Of the UN's five official languages, only French is unambiguously a European language as compared to Russian, Chinese, Arabic and the language of the Anglo-American world.

Because of the organisation's global reach, UN members collectively represent almost the whole of the world's population, led by China and India, each of which has 1.4 billion people. The collective population of Europe is a third of the size of these two gigantic Asian countries. The UN's diverse collection of high-income, middle-income and low-income countries account for virtually the whole of the world's GDP. Collectively, UN members account for the totality of the world's manmade greenhouse gases. While 93% of these gases originate outside Europe, they can nonetheless have a negative effect on the climate of Europe.

The inclusiveness of the United Nations is both an asset and a liability for decision-making. The charter of the United Nations gives it the right to deliberate on a wide range of global concerns, but neither the legal powers nor the economic resources to act effectively on its own. To do so, it requires a high degree of consensus and unanimity in the Security Council. Since the countries deemed to be the cause of military and economic threats are council members as well as those fearful for their security, unanimity is difficult to achieve (cf. Scott and Ku 2018).

The United Nations has nonetheless been able to take advantage of its global reach to focus attention on the threat of climate change. Its founding charter did not list protecting the environment as among its purposes. However, as scientific evidence and activist protests called attention to climate change as a threat to global security, it began to focus on the problem. In 1992 the United Nations Framework Convention on Climate Change (UNFCCC) was adopted to promote international co-operation to combat climate change. In 1997 its Kyoto Protocol set a series of targets for developed countries to reduce noxious emissions between 2008 and 2020. Its 2015 Paris Agreement set ambitious goals to limit the rise in global temperature by spending hundreds of billions of dollars that most member states have lacked the money or the political will to commit.

The UN Climate Change secretariat now services 198 countries nominally supporting its aims. A total of 29 annual Conferences of Parties on Climate Change have been held on different continents to discuss problems and stimulate national governments, civil society and private sector institutions to address the problem, albeit without significant material incentives or sanctions. Insofar as there is agreement, these conferences set standards and milestones for advancing actions to adopt climate-neutral processes that produce energy from the environment equal to the amount of energy that a society consumes (IPCC 2023).

Action on climate change requires the political will of governments to curtail, or ban their citizens from engaging in, activities that produce noxious emissions. The climate goals set out by the UN require massive sums for their achievement; the money is lacking in most countries that regularly participate in UN conferences on climate change. The 2024

Baku climate conference nearly broke down because of the immense demands of developing countries on highly developed countries for money to finance a large reduction in their polluting activities. There is also a collective action problem. Since most countries are not responsible for a substantial amount of climate change, measures adopted by a government the size of Ireland or Denmark would not be globally significant. Global change requires big polluting populous countries to adopt carbon–neutral policies. To date, there is not the widespread political will to curb emissions in the countries that are the biggest polluters, such as China, India and the United States.

Transactional alliances. Realist theories of international relations view alliances as transactional institutions in which national governments cooperate as long as it suits their own interest. By contrast, liberal theories emphasise that common interests lead national governments to join alliances to further collective goods such as international peace and prosperity. Theories of identity postulate that cultures and people who share a common sense of community may band together to protect themselves through collective action.

No European country has chosen to go it alone to deal with all three security threats, and only one country, Switzerland, has chosen to join just the UN. European states have sought to protect their military, economic and climate security through venue-shopping, that is, evaluating what different alliances have to offer to deal with particular security needs (cf. Chalmers and Iacobov 2023). The upshot is that more than three-quarters of Europe's countries are members of three alliances in order to deal with a variety of security threats, while retaining major powers to act on their own.

References

Chalmers, A. W. and Iacobov, A. A., 2023. The Stakes of Global Venue Shopping. In L. M. Dellmuth and E. A. Bloodgood, eds., *Advocacy Group Effects in Global Governance*, 197–228. London: Palgrave Macmillan.

Ewers-Peters, Nele Marianne, 2022. *Understanding EU–NATO Cooperation: How Member States Matter*. London: Routledge.

IPCC (Intergovernmental Panel on Climate Change), 2023. *Climate Change: Synthesis Report Summary for Policymakers*. Geneva: Intergovernmental Panel on Climate Change, https://doi.org/10.59327/IPCC/AR6-9789291691647.001.

Keukeleire, Stephan and Delreux, Tom, 2022. *The Foreign Policy of the European Union*, 3rd edn. London: Bloomsbury Academic.

Leuffen, Dirk, Rittberger, Berthold and Schimmelfennig, Frank, 2012. *Differentiated Integration*. London: Palgrave Macmillan.

Mayne, Richard, Pinder, J. and Roberts, J., 1990. *Federal Union: The Pioneers: A History of Federal Union*. Basingstoke: Macmillan.

Rieker, Pernille and Giske, Mathilde T. E., 2024. *European Actorness in a Shifting Political Order*. London: Palgrave Macmillan.

Rose, Richard, 2024. *Welfare Goes Global: Making Progress and Catching Up*. Oxford: Oxford University Press.

Scott, Shirley V. and Ku, Charlotte, eds., 2018. *Climate Change and the UN Security Council*. Cheltenham: Edward Elgar.

Teasdale, Anthony, 2016. *The Fouchet Plan: DeGaulle's Intergovernmental Design for Europe*. London: LSE Europe in Question Paper No.117.

CHAPTER 3

Public Opinion Matters

Abstract The accountability of a nation's governors to their electorate is an essential part of a democratic political system. If a government acts on its own there is a straight line of accountability from the electorate to government policymakers with feedback that can affect the government's electoral success. Alternatively, it can leverage its national resources by joining an alliance that collectively increases resources. It thus trades electoral accountability for greater effectiveness. Even if allies share a common goal, there will be national differences about how this goal can best be achieved and how costs are shared. Threats to the economy, the climate and war affect the lives of ordinary individuals as well as their government. Public knowledge of foreign policy is similar to public knowledge of domestic politics and can provide principles sufficient to justify popular judgements about going it alone or acting through an alliance to deal with big threats to security. The extent to which individuals divide in their views on security by personal characteristics or national context is shown by the eight-country European Security Survey of 12,685 respondents to interviews conducted after Russia's attack on Ukraine.

Keywords Opinion · Polls · Foreign policy · Security · Defence · Ukraine · Eurobarometer · European Union · NATO · UN

© The Author(s), under exclusive license to Springer Nature Switzerland AG 2025
B. Weßels and R. Rose, *European Public Opinion about Security*, Palgrave Studies in European Union Politics,
https://doi.org/10.1007/978-3-031-86263-2_3

The accountability of a nation's governors to their electorate is an essential part of a democratic political system (Schumpeter 1946: chapter 22; Bernhagen et al. 2019: 56). Citizens cast votes that give their government a mandate for policies and the authority to act effectively in response to unexpected security challenges. They can then hold the government accountable for the effectiveness of its actions at the next election. A critical feature of the security threats examined in this book is that they are foreign, that is, they originate from institutions and processes outside the boundaries of a nominally sovereign state. The outcome is determined by the interaction of a multiplicity of interdependent state and non-state actors that collectively have more resources to influence the outcome than a single state (Keohane and Nye 2011).

To deal with a trans-national threat to security, a government has the choice of acting on its own or working within an alliance. If it acts on its own there is a straight line of accountability from the electorate to government policymakers with feedback that can affect the government's electoral success and even support for the country's democratic institutions (Easton 1965). Alternatively, it can leverage its national resources by joining an alliance such as the European Union or NATO that collectively has far more resources. If it does so, a democratic government becomes more or less committed by a formal treaty to decisions made by a multi-national group (Johnson 2016). It thus trades electoral accountability for greater effectiveness. Even if allies share a common goal, such as winning a war, stopping global inflation or curbing climate change, there will be national differences about how this goal can best be achieved and how costs are shared.

An alliance has no electorate to which it is directly accountable. The undemocratic governments of most countries that belong to the United Nations are not accountable to their own citizens. The International Monetary Fund makes economic policy on the basis of decisions approved by a multi-national Executive Board casting votes that reflect their country's weight in the international economy. The European Union is unique in being a supra-national body with a popularly elected European Parliament. However, representation is on the basis of degressive proportionality: the smaller a country's population, the more its citizens are over-represented in EU institutions. There is thus a recurring demand to reduce the EU's democratic deficit (Piattoni 2015).

Since effective security and democratic accountability are both priorities, this creates a tension within government when the likelihood of a security threat increases. Even if governors do not see an immediate threat to their country's security, they may nonetheless join an alliance just in case things change. In untroubled times an alliance is unlikely to make serious demands on its members, so there is no chance of it coming into conflict with the views of national electorates. However, if a serious security threat arises, then there is a political cost in belonging to an alliance: national accountability is diminished by the need of governors to accept multi-national decisions.

Theories of democratic policymaking usually concentrate on domestic policies, thereby ignoring the tension between democratic accountability and national security. Political scientists have paid little attention to Robert Dahl's forecast (1989: 319f) that the internationalisation of political problems poses a threat to the accountability of democratic governments to their electorate. For example, Arend Lijphart (1999: 80f) found foreign policy issues of no importance politically in more than two-thirds of democratic party systems. Larry Diamond's (2008: 22) catalogue of democratic attributes includes the government controlling its own military and security services to avoid domestic subversion but does not deal with foreign military threats.

Theories of public opinion and foreign policy initially claimed that public opinion should not influence foreign policy because most citizens lack the necessary knowledge of foreign affairs (Lippmann 1922; Almond 1950). This view was complemented by the claim that political leaders and their elite advisers had the knowledge to make foreign policy decisions. Aaron Wildavsky (1966) went further, arguing that foreign policymaking should be free of politics. While a government should take conflicting political views into account in making domestic policies, Wildavsky declared this to be neither necessary nor desirable in foreign affairs because the president makes foreign policy in the national interest.

Empirical studies of major foreign policy decisions emphasise that problems are constructed, options reviewed and decisions made through a political process based on incomplete and sometimes inaccurate information and assumptions. From a study of the Cuban missile crisis, Graham Allison and Philip Zelikow (1999) generalised three competing perspectives, starting with a list of the imperfections in the rational actor model. There are also organisational biases due to the different types of knowledge and expertise of departments of foreign affairs, defence and finance. Moreover, leaders differ in the extent to which they want a decision-making structure that collectively provides competing views or just memos that support their own position. While these inherent limitations did not prevent Kennedy's Cuban missile policy from being successful, they were overwhelmingly present in Lyndon Johnson pursuing an unsuccessful war in Vietnam. Post-1945 European leaders have avoided being responsible for a major military defeat by avoiding engaging in war. Exceptionally, British prime minister Tony Blair did commit the United Kingdom to fight alongside the United States and suffered defeat in the Iraq War.

Democratic principles do not require that the mass of the public has the same political knowledge as policymakers or a given level of education to be eligible to vote. Public knowledge of foreign policy has been found to be similar to public knowledge of domestic politics (Baum and Potter 2015). Public opinion based on general principles rather than detailed knowledge can be sufficient to justify popular judgements about security choices (Kertzer and Zeitzoff 2017).

Since threats to the economy, the climate and war affect individuals as well as their government, the next section examines different ways in which security conditions can affect the lives of ordinary Europeans. When international developments stimulate a sense of insecurity, people can either expect their government to deal with security challenges on its own or alternatively support belonging to an alliance. The second section sets out models that identify the influences that lead individuals to differ in how they see national security choices. To determine which influences are most important empirically, we analyse public opinion data in the eight-country European Security survey; it is described in the concluding section of this chapter.

3.1 How Security Matters at the Grassroots

Ordinary Europeans face dozens of potential threats to their security. Many arise from problems at home that they can do something about. If an intruder breaks a window in their house, they can repair the window and install a burglar alarm. If their pay leaves them short of money, they can ask their employer for a pay rise, seek a second part-time job or cut spending on non-essential goods and services. However, when threats arise to national security, there is little that individuals can do to protect their country from an attack from abroad.

Ordinary Europeans have no need to monitor foreign relations as long as they do not perceive threats to their own security; they can concentrate their political attention on domestic issues or ignore politics entirely. In normal circumstances the government has no reason to prompt citizens to focus on security threats. This can cause ordinary people to worry about their security instead of maintaining a passive confidence that their government is doing its job effectively. However, when action is needed to protect security, for example, raising spending on defence substantially to meet targets set by NATO, the costs cannot easily be hidden from the public.

When the impact of insecurity is felt at the grassroots, for example, food prices rising as a result of global inflation, people will blame the government if it does not do something. The extent to which individuals become aware of threats to their security depends on whether the threat affects a persisting concern, as in the case of economic conditions, or an intermittent one, like the threat of military action (see Sect. 1.2). Awareness varies with the visibility of a threat: Climate change strikes home if successive years of drought kill a farmer's crops. As long as the impact of a threat at the grassroots is low, then the general public may become aware of it only if it is publicised by activists raising the issue in the media, as has happened with climate change, or when dramatic international events occur, such as the Russian invasion of Ukraine.

Economic Insecurity. National governments routinely assess economic conditions by monitoring national and global macroeconomic indicators. While the government monitors foreign exchange rates for the country's currency, these are rarely noticed by Europeans, especially since the introduction of the euro. When trade conditions are good, most people do not care where a car was made, but how it drives and how much it costs.

Many national economic measures are constructed by aggregating large numbers of statistics into a single figure such as the country's GDP. Even though it is measured in money terms, no one has ever seen the billions of euros that constitute a European country's GDP. Price indexes conflate into a single index number the prices of a notional basket of goods that reflect the purchases of an average consumer, but half of voters differ to a significant degree from the average. Unemployment statistics refer to a condition that individuals may face if their employer starts laying off workers. However, about half the population cannot be directly affected since they are outside the labour force as home workers, students or retired. In the course of the year unemployment directly affects only a limited minority of adults.

Individuals do not need to pay attention to politics to be aware of whether their economic conditions are satisfactory. When they go shopping for food or buy petrol for their car, the numbers that flash up at the checkout counter will tell them whether prices are rising. When viewing their bank statement, they will see whether their income has matched their expenditure and the message of deteriorating conditions will be reinforced if they cannot pay their monthly credit card bill in full. Interest rates are abstract numbers that are given meaning on the doorstep only when people seek a mortgage to buy a house. They need not listen to a government minister blaming the rising cost of living on activities in the global economy that are outside the government's control. When they feel the pinch of economic insecurity, Europeans can place the blame on a national government that had previously taken credit for prosperity.

Climate Change. International evidence of climate change is cited with scientific precision. Past and future changes in the global temperature are reported in one one-hundredth of 1 °C. The timescale for assessing climate change extends over centuries. The EU's European Environmental Agency (2023: Fig. 1) reports that European temperatures have been rising since 1850 due to the effects of industrialisation and the rate of change has increased since 1900. It estimates that European temperatures in the decade ending in 2022 were from 2.04 to 2.10 °C warmer than they were almost 175 years earlier. It noted that in the most recent half-century the world was warming at a higher rate than at any time in the past two thousand years.

Wherever people live, weather is always visible and is often the subject of conversation. Individuals build up expectations of what weather ought to be like at different times of year and what is considered normal. Grassroots climate expectations vary with the age of individuals. Ideas about climate change may be based on subjective recollections of what the climate was like when people were young. They can also be based on information from the media, which reports not only scientific statements about the climate but also competing views of partisan activists. Social media can circulate unevaluated claims denying or forecasting climate disaster.

The UN Framework Convention on Climate Change has set a target of limiting global climate change to less than 2 °C above the pre-industrial level by 2050. It now forecasts that, in the absence of action to curb the causes of global warming, the limit will be exceeded before that date as climate change in Europe has been greater than the global average. Collectively, American estimates can vary from the Environmental Protection Agency's cost of just under $200 billion to more than $1 trillion according to economists (Economist 2024).

An inevitable consequence of adopting policies to reduce future climate change is that political costs are front-end loaded. They include taxes on energy products to discourage use; economic incentives to install solar panels or renewable energy heating; and replacing automobiles fuelled by petrol or diesel with electric vehicles. However, benefits arrive far beyond the lifetime of the government of the day. In European democracies, politicians can seek popularity by inveighing against climate regulations on the grounds that the costs are too high or by threatening that the cost of inaction will have worse consequences.

Military Threats. The history of Europe is a story of wars great and small. However, the vast majority of Europeans have lived in an era when their country has not been at war. Thus, they have no first-hand experience of the impact of military actions that affect the lives of everyone in a society, and can kill or maim hundreds of thousands of people. While a national government maintains a peacetime defence ministry just in case fighting breaks out, the ministry is usually of secondary importance to the government's domestic policies and of little interest to the media.

The Russian invasion of Ukraine in February 2022 has brought home to European governments that, although the Cold War with the Soviet Union is no more, Moscow is once again a military threat. National governments are sending money and materials to Ukraine to fight a proxy war to deter Russian aggression. They are also under pressure from Washington to meet their defence spending targets. The return of Donald Trump to the White House means that they can no longer be confident of the United States committing troops to engage with Russia in the event Moscow carries out a carefully calculated act of aggression against a NATO member state.

Europeans are reminded that war has returned to their near abroad by almost daily televised reports of the progress of the war in Ukraine and the damage that has been done to Ukrainian cities. Interviews with those who have lost their homes or their husband or son show the human cost of war. Ukrainian flags are displayed in many public places to show European solidarity, and countries have accommodated several million Ukrainian refugees as their homeland has become a battleground. Indirectly, the

Kremlin's weaponisation of its energy exports has driven up the cost of energy for tens of millions of European households and contributed to global inflation.

Whether people see their country facing a serious threat of military attack is likely to be affected by its past history and geography. In countries that were once part of a Moscow-led military alliance enforced by Soviet troops on their territory, the threat of Russian military action is not far away in time or space. By contrast, in countries further west such as Italy, it appears relatively remote. Moreover, for people who lack the education or the political interest to follow news from abroad on television, there is no stimulus to think about a military threat to their own lives. Lack of interest can rapidly be reversed when the threat of war comes to their country, a family member is called up for military service or diggers start fitting out an air raid shelter at the end of their street.

3.2 A Model of Individual Security Choices

Two critical questions must be answered whenever an issue of security arises. How much of a threat is it to national security? Should the government deal with the threat on its own or by joining a multi-national alliance?

State-centric theories of security tend to assume an undivided national interest yielding a single answer. However, public opinion in a democracy is invariably divided. Even if there is a consensus among policymakers about a major security issue, voters may disagree. Referendums show that this is the case when a government decides to join the European Union (Rose 2020). While a majority normally endorse the decision of their governors, the margin of victory can be small. Moreover, majorities in Norway and Switzerland have rejected agreements their leaders have negotiated with Brussels, and in 2016 a majority of British voters endorsed Brexit, the United Kingdom leaving the European Union.

Individual perceptions of threats to security are not determined by government policies; they are subjective political judgements that individuals construct from their own experiences and information at hand (cf. Checkel 1998; Wendt 1995). If citizens do not see a threat to national security, there is no need to accept limits on their government's accountability. This creates a political bias in favour of a government shying away from interpreting a trans-national activity as a security threat if doing so would create unwelcome political costs. For example, many governments have hesitated to accept demands of green activists to adopt policies that would disrupt the behaviour of motorists or greatly increase the cost of heating homes. However, if citizens see a substantial security risk, they may be more disposed to accept the costs of increasing expenditure to protect their security.

Perception of Threats. Even though collective security threats affect all Europeans, people differ from each other in the extent to which they see their country facing threats. Figures 3.1 and 3.2 present summary models identifying major types of influences in both national contexts and characteristics specific to individuals, which can influence whether an individual perceives a security issue as a relatively high or low threat to national security.

The history of a country is embedded in a national context shared by all its citizens. For individuals, relatively recent history is most important, that is, developments that they have experienced in their own life or that have altered their family's history with a lasting effect. While only the oldest of Europeans have a direct experience of the Second World War, tens of millions of people have experienced living under a communist regime subject to control from Moscow until it collapsed just over three decades ago. This experience contrasts with that of European citizens who have lived in democratic societies offering both freedom and a much higher standard of living than a communist regime. Population size, which varies greatly between European countries, has a wide impact on resources that can affect individual views of threats to national security.

In every European society individuals differ in their political attitudes and in their status in the socio-economic structure in ways that influence their political perceptions. Generations of political science researchers

National context   *Individual*   *Perception of threat*

History ⇨ Political attitudes ⇨

High – Low

Resources ⇨ Socioeconomic status ⇗

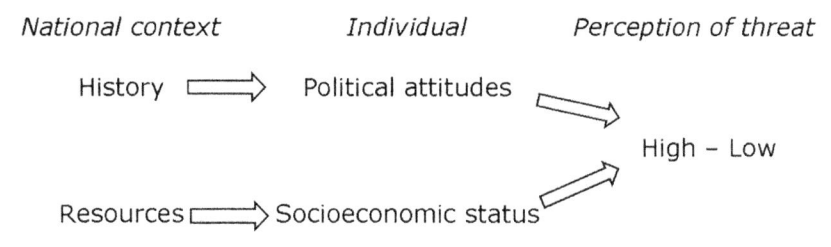

Fig. 3.1 A model of individual perceptions of threats

```
National context          Individual              Choice
                    ┌─────────────────────┐  ┌─────────────────┐
      History  ⇒    │    Sees threat      │  │  On our own     │
                    │  Political attitudes│⇒ │      or         │
      Resources ⇒   │                     │  │     ally        │
                    │ Socioeconomic status│  │  EU, NATO, UN   │
                    └─────────────────────┘  └─────────────────┘
```

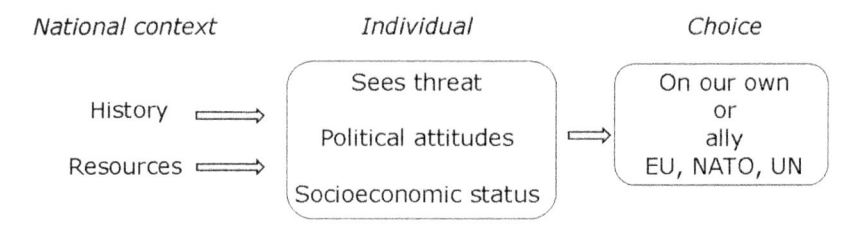

Fig. 3.2 A model of choice or rejection of an alliance

have documented the importance of left/right ideology in differentiating political views. The growth of populist parties suggests that major differences in democratic values divide voters. National values about sovereignty, foreign trade and immigration are relevant to foreign affairs and divide Europeans. Sociological research emphasises that differences in income and education give individuals a socio-economic status that can affect how they perceive political issues. Since generations differ in their first-hand knowledge of their country's history, this can create different perceptions of risk among younger and older Europeans.

If Europeans do perceive a substantial threat to their security from military, economic or climate conditions, then they face a choice about what should be done. Should their government deal with it on its own or should it turn to one of the alliances to which it belongs—the EU, NATO or the UN—for help? The second figure differs from the preceding model. First of all, it sorts people into two groups: those who have no need for a choice since they do not regard a security issue as a significant threat. Secondly, among those who do see an issue as a threat, there is a choice between going it alone or turning to an alliance to gain effectiveness. If the latter is the case, individuals can make their first choice between multiple alliances to which their government belongs.

The models provide the theoretical base for a pair of broad hypotheses:

H 1 Differences in national context cause variations in individual perceptions of threats and choice of allies.

H 2 Differences in political and socio-economic attitudes cause variations in individual perceptions of threats and choice of allies.

Although differing in emphasis, the above hypotheses are complementary rather than in conflict. The first hypothesis takes into account the likelihood that individuals similar in their attitudes and status may differ politically if they are citizens of countries differing in population or in their experience of communist control. The second hypothesis takes into account the fact that people who live in a democratic societies differ in their political opinions.

Because the models are generic, they can be applied to a variety of security threats. However, security studies emphasise categoric differences between threats from the global economy, military action and climate change (see e.g. Buzan and Hansen 2009). This suggests that differences between threats may produce differences in how individuals perceive threats and alliances. However, theories of political psychology emphasise that how people perceive and make choices reflects an individual's generic predispositions rather than discriminating on the basis of specific details of threats. Therefore, the third hypothesis is:

H 3 Whatever the security threat, influences on individual perceptions and threats will remain the same.

The extent to which empirical evidence supports these hypotheses will be tested in Chapters 4 and 5.

3.3 THE EUROPEAN SECURITY SURVEY

To test hypotheses about how individuals perceive security threats, we need public opinion data that includes indicators usually divided between separate surveys about domestic and international politics. To ensure that our conclusions apply to different types of security threats, a survey that focuses on a single threat such as Russia's invasion of Ukraine is not suitable. This point is particularly relevant given Russia's readiness to weaponise economic means to destabilise European countries. There is also a need for respondents to be given a choice of allies rather than being asked exclusively about a single ally, as is done in Eurobarometer surveys that offer the EU as the only source of help to national governments (cf. Höpner and Jurczyk 2015). To test whether conclusions are independent of national context, we require comparable data from multiple European countries.

The European Security Survey (EuroSec) meets all the requirements for comparatively testing attitudes towards security. The EuroSec questionnaire included indicators of attitudes towards all three types of security risk and potential allies for dealing with risks. It also included independent variables suitable for testing the three hypotheses about why security attitudes vary (see Appendix for more details of the survey's variables). A total of 12,685 people were interviewed online in eight

European countries between 29 November and 18 December 2022. At this time the war in Ukraine was challenging Europe's defence, inflation had abruptly spiked in the global economy, and it was shortly after a major UN conference on climate change. The choice of countries was determined by the EuroSec questions being part of an omnibus survey of the Cluster of Excellence Contestations of the Liberal Script research programme of seven Berlin social science institutes funded by the German Science Foundation (Giebler et al. 2022).

The eight countries in the EuroSec survey—Germany, the United Kingdom, Hungary, Italy, Poland, Romania, Sweden and Croatia—belong to multiple alliances. All belong to the United Nations and NATO and, except for the United Kingdom, belong to the European Union. They also differ substantially in their resources. Four countries have a big population, while four are smaller in population (Table 3.1). They also differ in the living standards of their citizens. The nominal Gross Domestic Product per capita of Sweden and Germany is more than three-fifths larger than Croatia and Romania. The national capitals of EuroSec countries vary too in their vulnerability to Russian military aggression, as indicated by their distance from Moscow. London and Rome are about twice as far away from the Russian capital as are Warsaw and Stockholm. Difference in the kilotons of carbon dioxide that countries contribute to global pollution reflect the extent of industry as well as population and GDP. The United Kingdom and Poland are each relatively high in emissions, while Sweden and Croatia are relatively low.

Since we are interested in the collective choices of Europeans, the following chapters report the views of respondents in total rather than subdividing responses into separate columns for each country. The evidence justifies doing so, since respondents in each country are divided in their views in response to every question asked. To say that Britons or Germans as a whole hold a given view suppresses the evidence of divisions within nations, which tend to be greater than divisions between nations. Multi-level regression equations show the extent to which individual political attitudes and socio-economic characteristics account for differences among Europeans. The inclusion of measures of political, economic and social characteristics tests the influence of national differences. In their response to threats to security, Europeans tend to differ more according to their individual characteristics than their national passports.

Table 3.1 European countries differ in resources

Country	Population in mill.	GDP per capita, PPP, 2021	Distance capital from Moscow in km	Warming 2022 in C.
Germany	83.2	53,180	1,608	2.59
United Kingdom	67.3	44,979	2,500	1.91
Italy	59.1	41,929	2,376	2.16
Poland	37.7	34,916	1,150	2.04
Romania	19.1	30,777	1,498	1.83
Sweden	10.4	53,613	1,227	2.14
Hungary	9.7	33,593	1,569	2.10
Croatia	3.8	31,636	1,867	2.29

Sources Population: Eurostat. *GDP per capita, PPP, 2021*: World Bank
Distance capital to Moscow: own calculations. *Warming*: Food and Agriculture Organization of the United Nations (FAO). 2022. FAOSTAT Climate Change, Climate Indicators, Temperature change. Annual estimates of mean surface temperature change measured with respect to a baseline climatology, corresponding to the period 1951–1980

REFERENCES

Allison, Graham and Zelikow, Philip, 1999. *Essence of Decision*, 2nd edn. New York: Longman.
Almond, Gabriel, 1950. *The American People and Foreign Policy*. New York: Harcourt, Brace and Company.
Baum, Matthew A. and Potter, Philip B. K., 2015. *War and Democratic Constraint: How the Public Influences Foreign Policy*. Princeton: Princeton University Press.
Bernhagen, Patrick, 2019. Measuring Democracy and Democratization. In Christian Haerpfer et al., ed., *Democratization*, 2nd edn, 52–66. Oxford: Oxford University Press.
Buzan, Barry and Hansen, Lene, 2009. *The Evolution of International Security Studies*. Cambridge: Cambridge University Press.
Checkel, Jeffrey, 1998. 'The Constructivist Turn in International Relations Theory', *World Politics*, 50, 2, 324–348.
Dahl, Robert A., 1989. *Democracy and Its Critics*. New Haven: Yale University Press.
Diamond, Larry, 2008. *The Spirit of Democracy*. New York: Times Books.
Easton, David, 1965. *A Systems Analysis of Political Life*. New York: John Wiley.
Economist, 2024. Multi-Melting Problems, 1 June.
European Environmental Agency, 2023. *Global and European Temperatures: Analysis and Data; Indicators*. Copenhagen: www.eea.europa.eu.

Giebler, Heiko, Hellmeier, S., Keremoglu, E., Gerschweksi, J. and Zuern, M., 2022. *Contestations of the Liberal Script*. Berlin: Cluster of Excellence EXC 2055 Project-ID: 390715649.

Höpner, Martin and Jurczyk, Bojan, 2015. How the Eurobarometer Blurs the Line between Research and Propaganda, *MPIfG Discussion Paper, No. 15/6*. Cologne: Max Planck Institute for the Study of Societies.

Johnson, Jesse C., 2016. 'Alliance Treaty Obligations and War Intervention', *Conflict Management and Peace Sciences*, 33, 5, 451–468.

Keohane, Robert O. and Nye, Joseph, 2011. *Power and Interdependence*, 4th edn. New York: Longman.

Kertzer, J. D. and Zeitzoff, T., 2017. 'A Bottom-Up Theory of Public Opinion about Foreign Policy', *American Journal of Political Science*, 61, 3, 543–558.

Lijphart, Arend, 1999. *Patterns of Democracy*. New Haven: Yale University Press.

Lippmann, Walter, 1922. *Public Opinion*. New York: Macmillan.

Piattoni, Simona, ed., 2015. *The European Union: Democratic Principles and Institutional Architectures in Times of Crisis*. Oxford: Oxford Academic.

Rose, Richard, 2020. *How Referendums Challenge European Democracy*. London: Palgrave Macmillan

Schumpeter, Joseph A., 1946. *Capitalism, Socialism and Democracy*, 4th edn. London: George Allen and Unwin.

Wendt, Alexander, 1995. 'Constructing International Politics', *International Security*, 20, 1, 71–81.

Wildavsky, Aaron, 1966. 'The Two Presidencies', *Transaction/Society*, 4, 7–14.

CHAPTER 4

Sizing Up Threats

Abstract European democracies need the support of their citizens not only at the ballot box but also through co-operation in implementing public policies. To mobilise popular support for security policies, governments need their citizens to see that their country faces substantial threats to its security. This will make ordinary people more likely to accept giving security policies priority over popular social policies. The task is easier to accomplish when the threat hits people directly, such as global inflation. It can be harder when the threat is distant in space, as Russian aggression in Ukraine is for many Europeans. Threats may also be distant in time, such as dire changes in the climate in 2050. Accountability to voters provides an incentive for politicians to make ordinary people aware of threats rather than hiding them, only to be caught out by events revealing their failure. The European Security Survey assesses the extent to which the general public is attentive to risks to their country's security from the global economy, military action and climate change. Regression analyses find that within every country people divide according to their political attitudes and socio-economic status.

Keywords Security · Threats · Opinion · War · Inflation · Climate · European Union · NATO · UN

European democracies need the support of their citizens not only at the ballot box but also through co-operation in implementing public policies. For instance, reducing carbon emissions requires wholesale changes in the way that people heat their homes and use their automobile or public transport. Combating inflation requires individuals to accept limited increases in pay when prices are rising fast in order to avoid a wage–price spiral that pushes inflation higher. To deter the threat of military aggression, citizens must accept being liable for military service, paying higher taxes to finance military expenditure or both.

In order to mobilise popular support for costly security policies, governments need their citizens to see that their country faces substantial threats to its security. This will make ordinary people more likely to accept giving security policies priority over popular social policies. The task is easier when the threat hits people directly, such as global inflation reducing the real income of households. It can be harder when the threat is distant in space, as Russian aggression in Ukraine is for many West Europeans. Threats may also be distant in time, such as disturbing changes in the climate in 2050. Accountability to voters provides an incentive for politicians to make ordinary people aware of threats rather than hiding such facts only to be caught out by events revealing their failure to protect national security.

Opinion surveys can assess the extent to which the general public is attentive to risks to their country's security. The next section presents EuroSec data showing the extent to which Europeans see their country facing substantial threats from the global economy, military action and climate change. It is followed by an analysis of the influences that divide people between those who do and do not see their country facing substantial threats to their security today.

4.1 Perceptions of Global Threats

Even though European governments see threats to national security, ordinary people remote from government may not have the same awareness. To guard against creating opinions about security threats where they do not already exist (Converse 1964), the European Security Survey starts by asking about respondents' perceptions of possible threats. *How much do you think this country is at risk from problems in the global economy, military threats and climate change?* For each potential threat, respondents were asked to choose between four alternatives: *a big risk, a fair amount of risk, not much risk* or *no risk*. If an individual answered *don't know* or *I prefer not to say*, this was also coded.

An overwhelming majority of Europeans do have views about national security. Only 6% say they have no opinion about the global economy, 8% have no opinion about military action and 5% express no opinion about climate change. The small size of these groups means that policymakers cannot count on a lot of passive support, since more than nine-tenths of their citizens have an opinion one way or another about the extent of security threats.

In evaluating the scale of risk, Europeans discriminate between different types of security (Table 4.1). At the time of the EuroSec survey, European economies had experienced a spurt of growth in reaction to the downturn caused by the Covid pandemic. Nonetheless, 88% of Europeans still saw the global economy as posing a substantial threat, that is, seeing a big or fair risk. Negative effects of climate change are not forecast to become apparent for decades, but four-fifths saw a substantial risk from climate change. Even though the Russian invasion of Ukraine had occurred almost a year before EuroSec interviews were conducted, under half of respondents saw military action as a substantial threat to their country. It is possible that this low sense of threat reflects some Europeans having a denial mechanism that encourages them to believe that unwelcome events can't happen here.

The majority of Europeans are moderate in their judgements. People see security risks as being fairly large or not very large rather than a big risk or no risk. This middle-of-the-road view is held by 55% about risks

Table 4.1 How Europeans see risks to national security

Q. How much do you think your country is at risk from

	Global economy (%)	Military action (%)	Climate change (%)
Big risk	43.1	15.0	40.1
Fair amount	45.2	33.6	39.9
(Substantial)	(88.3)	(48.6)	(80.1)
Not much risk	10.3	42.8	15.8
No risk	1.4	8.7	4.1
(Low risk)	(11.7)	(51.4)	(19.9)
$N = 100\%$	11,919	11,604	12,024

Source European Security Survey, 2022

from the global economy, 56% as regards climate change and 76% about military action. The median respondent sees a fair amount of risk in the global economy and from climate change, but not much risk of military action.

Among Europeans who make judgements about security, the largest group, 40%, consistently feel insecure, seeing a substantial threat to security from the global economy, military action and climate change. They may be described as being prepared for all kinds of troubles in a troubled world. In the middle are those who see at least one fair-sized or big risk and at least one area with little or no risk. Given the current state of world affairs, the 4% of Europeans who consistently see little or no threat to their country's security can be described as overconfident.

4.2 Who Sees Their Security Threatened?

Europeans can decide whether each type of security is a high or low risk on the basis of particular features of the problem. Insofar as this is the case, we would expect the influences that affect the perception of risk to vary between security types. Alternatively, the perceptions of individuals may be more influenced by what shapes their general outlook on society. If this is the case, since an individual's characteristics remain constant during a survey, statistically significant influences would remain the same for perceptions of economic, military and climate risk.

Our generic model of how individuals see risks (Fig. 3.1) postulates that differences in perceptions reflect the combined influence of national history and resources and of individual attitudes and socio-economic status. Statistically, risk can be expressed as a function of these four influences plus an error term that stands for everything that the regression does not include or identify as significant:

$$Risk\ perception\ (f)\ History,\ Resources,\ Attitudes,\ Status + e$$

We use ordinary least-squares regression to identify the absolute and relative strength of hypothesised influences of national context and individual characteristics. We calculate separate regressions for threats from the global economy, military action and climate change in order to test whether the influences are consistently significant or differ between these three problems. Given 12,685 respondents in our pooled multi-national data set, the level of statistical significance is set at $p < 0.001$ (**) for individual indicators and at $p < 0.050$ (*) for national context indicators.

Statistical significance leaves open how much impact an influence has on the perception of risk. Since independent variables differ in range, we have standardised them on a common scale of 0 to 1, in which 1 is a measure of the strongest endorsement of an ordinal measure, for example, the importance of democracy or national sovereignty, or the last in a series of alternatives, for example, strongly right-wing. The marginal effect of each independent variable is calculated from the regression coefficients. The size of the marginal effect shows how much the perception of a given risk alters between the lowest value, no risk, and big risk, after controlling for the effect of all other variables. If there is a negative sign for a coefficient, this shows it reduces the perception of risk. The absence of a sign shows the influence is positive; for example, the more people see democracy as important, the more they are likely to perceive economic and climate change risks. Full details of all variables in the regressions are reported in the appendix.

Contextual Influences on Risk Perception. While all states have a claim to equality under international law, when it comes to protecting national security, differences in national resources can influence the extent to which individuals perceive their country as being at risk (see Table 3.1). Since security threats differ in kind, for each type we test the effect of a context measure specially relevant to the risk.

While national economies differ in size, all are part of the global economy and therefore vulnerable to its effect. Theoretically, the stronger a country's economy, the less likely its citizens should be to see the global economy as a big risk. In the regression analysis its strength is indicated by its gross domestic product per capita controlling for differences in national purchasing power, since individual economic security depends on what individuals can buy in their home market. Regression analysis shows the national economy is significant; the higher a country's GDP per capita, the less likely people are to see the global economy as a substantial risk.

Even though Russian aggression in Ukraine has not involved the armed forces of a NATO or an EU member state, it has brought home to European governments that while the Cold War with the Soviet Union has ended, Moscow once again poses a threat to their national security. There are daily media reports of the damage that Ukraine has suffered in the proxy war that it is fighting on behalf of European countries.

The extent to which this makes people see their country facing a military threat is likely to be influenced by their geographical and historical context. Regression analysis confirms that the further a country is from Moscow, the less likely its citizens are to see their country facing a big military threat. The marginal effect of this context variable is stronger than that of any individual characteristic. While a country's communist past has a statistically significant effect, its effect is less than its current distance from Moscow.

For the third threat, climate change, one can expect that the higher the extent of global warming in a country, the more likely citizens would be to see climate change as a substantial threat to their security. Climate change can be measured by the extent of national warming from one year to the next. However, the regression analysis shows the opposite: the statistically significant marginal effect of global warming is negative. The higher the level of global warming in a country, the less likely people are to see climate change as a big threat to their security.

Political Attitudes Vary in Influence. Within every European society, individuals differ in their social attitudes and their socio-economic status. Hypothesis 2 predicts that individual differences have a substantial effect on perceptions of risk independently of national context. However, this leaves open which particular attitudes measured in the EuroSec survey have a significant influence.

While everyone who lives in a European democracy is obligated to comply with its laws, everyone is not required to place the same value on democracy. This is shown by replies to the EuroSec question: *How important is it to you to live in a country governed democratically?* On a 0- to 10-point scale, 58% see living in a democracy as absolutely important, giving it the highest score. In addition 19% place the importance of democracy at point 8 or 9 and an additional 11% place it at 6 or 7, above the midpoint.

We would expect that people who see democracy as being more important would be more likely to see threats to the security of their political system. This is especially the case for the perception of climate change as a threat. The marginal effect, 0.553, is the highest of the seven significant influences on seeing climate change as a big risk (Table 4.2). The importance given to democracy is significant for the global economy too, but the marginal effect is half that of climate change. The value placed on democracy has no effect on the perception of military threats.

Table 4.2 Influences on perception of risks

Risk low (1) to high (4)	Economy (coeff.)	Military (coeff.)	Climate (coeff.)
Democracy important	0.235***	−0.037	0.553***
Left_Right	0.047	0.038	−0.358***
Immigration danger	−0.027	0.116***	−0.336***
National sovereignty	0.158***	0.237***	−0.214***
Protection from imports	0.009	0.188***	0.226***
Living standard	−0.259***	−0.191***	−0.107*
Positive nat'l economy	−0.732***	−0.214***	−0.031
Education	−0.007	−0.055	−0.083*
Political interest	0.164***	0.104*	0.030
Young (under 30)	0.027	−0.014	0.010
Older (over 64)	−0.138***	−0.119***	−0.021
GDP per cap. PPP	−0.146***		
Distance capital to Moscow		−0.266***	
Global warming			−0.267***
Intercept	3.335***	2.487***	3.218***
Number of observations	7669	7578	7685
Pseudo R^2	0.129	0.051	0.088

*** $p < 0.001$, * $p < 0.050$ Multi-level logistic regression
Independent variables normalised (0 minimum, 1 maximum)
Source European Security Survey, 2022

Ideological differences between left-wing and right-wing outlooks influence divisions in voting. However, because national security is collective, there may be non-partisan agreement. The theoretical implication of being on the left or right is debatable. Arguably, the left is more likely to see society divided by conflicts, making those on the left more likely to perceive threats to security. Yet insofar as those on the right favour conserving traditional conditions, this could make them more sensitive to security threats. Opposing ideological pressures tend to cancel out; they lack a significant effect on seeing risks from military action or the global economy. However, there is a substantial effect on the perception of climate change. A more right-wing outlook significantly reduces the likelihood of seeing climate change as a threat. The greater readiness of the left to see threats to the climate may reflect a distrust of the activities of profit-making industries that are major polluters.

Nationalist values have a logical link with national security. Since a common theme of populist parties is that foreign influences threaten the country in many ways (Mudde, 2016), people holding nationalist views should be more likely to see threats to their national security. The EuroSec survey asked whether people agreed or disagreed with three nationalist statements.

In reply to the statement *International organisations are taking away too much power from this country's government*, 51% expressed a degree of agreement compared to 31% who tended to disagree. As predicted, those who react against international organisations are significantly more likely to see military threats and risks from the global economy. However, they are less likely to see climate change as a threat, a view that may be due to nationalists ignoring an issue seen as promoted by activist organisations.

The EuroSec question about immigration—*Immigrants endanger our society by bringing new ideas and cultures*—explicitly emphasises a cultural threat. Notwithstanding widespread European concern about immigration issues, most respondents did not go so far as to see it endangering their society. The median group, 16% of the total, took an in-between position on a 7-point scale, while 44% saw immigration as endangering their society and 39% disagreed. The debate about immigration being an economic asset, whatever its cultural effects, appears to have neutralised its potential effect on perceptions of the global economy; it is not significant. However, the more people see immigration as a cultural threat, the more likely they are to see substantial threats to national security from military action.

When EuroSec respondents were offered the statement *This country should limit the import of foreign products in order to protect its national economy*, 53% tended to agree, almost twice the 28% who tended to disagree. Consistent with political discourse describing trade with China as a threat to defence as well as to the economy, those holding protectionist views are significantly more likely to see international trade as a risk to military defence and global climate change. By contrast, foreign trade is not regarded as a significant threat to the national economy. This suggests that the EU's creation of a single European market of 27 countries has led European consumers to accept foreign products, whether coming from within Europe or from more distant countries.

Influence of Socio-economic Status Varies. Sociological theories emphasise the influence of an individual's status on their political opinions. The generic proposition 'It's the economy, stupid' asserts that material interests are important. However, there is no agreement about whether economic or social class indicators are more important. Moreover, education is increasingly seen as a better measure of individual status and, of special relevance here, of greater understanding of foreign countries. Increased education is also linked to generational differences. Older generations have had much more experience than younger Europeans of times when national security was at risk, whereas younger Europeans have been socialised to take for granted crossing national borders easily and mixing with people of different nationalities.

Economic status can be measured by income, occupation or an individual's self-assessment. There are difficulties in using income to create a hierarchy since individual incomes can be pooled in a household. The obstacle becomes fundamental in cross-national comparisons, since earnings that confer low status in one country may confer higher status in another. Therefore, the EuroSec Survey asks respondents to describe their standard of living subjectively on a seven-point scale ranging from poor to rich. A total of 40% place themselves at the midpoint of this hierarchy, 21% one point above the midpoint and 23% one point below.

Theoretically, those who are economically better-off have the most to lose from threats to national security and could therefore be most attentive to security threats. On the other hand, the economic security of people who are better-off may allow them to feel insulated from national political problems and therefore less concerned about risks to national security. The regression analyses support the latter theory. People who see themselves as being better-off than average are less likely to see significant threats to their country from the global economy and from military action. Being better-off does not significantly affect the perception of a threat from climate change.

When people evaluate the economy, they make judgements about both their personal situation and the state of the national economy; both judgements may influence their political opinions (Kinder and Kiewiet 1981; Lockerbie 2006). When the EuroSec Survey was fielded at the end of 2022, the effects of the COVID-19 pandemic had not disappeared. Hence, when asked to evaluate their country's current economic performance, 62% made negative responses as against 21% seeing the economy performing positively. Being positive had a very big marginal effect on reducing the perception of a threat from the global economy and a significant but lesser effect on military risks.

The spread of mass higher education throughout Europe has created a new status hierarchy based on educational achievement. In addition to education affecting voting independently of economic class, it also creates divisions between cosmopolitan views and nationalist opinions. Given cross-national differences in how educational status is conferred, the EuroSec survey classifies educational achievement in three basic categories: low, medium and high. A total of 55% of Europeans have a medium education. The 30% with a higher education are now double the size of those with only a low education.

People with more education should have more knowledge about security threats facing their country. At the time of the EuroSec survey, both expert opinion and media reports were calling attention to a relatively high risk of a global recession, Russia was at war in Ukraine and Europe had had its warmest October on record. Nonetheless, people with more education were not significantly more likely to see threats from the global economy or military action.

People who are interested in politics are likely to know more about major problems facing their government, including challenges to national security. The motives for becoming interested are multiple and, like voting, do not require a higher education. On a seven-point scale ranging from not at all interested to very interested in politics, the majority of EuroSec respondents place themselves above the midpoint, and one-sixth say they are very interested in politics. Being interested in politics significantly increases a sense of the global economy as a threat, but not the other security risks (Table 4.2).

The political experience of youths differs from generation to generation. The current generation of older Europeans was being socialised politically when a global recession unexpectedly struck Europe in 1975. For middle-age Europeans, the end of the Cold War with the fall of the Berlin Wall and the Soviet Union was a major event. Today's youthful generation had the unique experience of being made aware of global risks by the COVID pandemic. Given these differences, regression equations include two distinctive generational cohorts at opposite ends of the age continuum, young adults below the age of 30 and older adults age 65 or higher.

Older Europeans are significantly less likely than average to see the global economy and military action as causing substantial threats to national security. This suggests that people who are living on a pension do not share the anxieties about the global economy of Europeans of working age, since they have a secure income and are not at risk of unemployment because they are retired. Moreover, they are less likely to see a substantial military threat today, perhaps because European cities do not show the scars of wars as cities still did when they were growing up after the Second World War. Young people do not differ significantly in their perception of security risks from the bulk of Europeans, who are middle-aged (Table 4.2).

Most Important Influences on Perceptions of Risk. In our generic models, Hypothesis 3 postulates that influences on security perceptions will be consistent, having the same effect, significant or null, on all three types of risks. However, the regression equations in Table 4.2 show that this is not the case: the great majority of influences are selective, sometimes having a significant effect and sometimes not. Of the 11 individual variables included, only the measure of national sovereignty consistently has a significant influence on all three security risks, albeit not always in the same direction (Table 4.2). Similarly, only two variables, youth and education, consistently fail to achieve significance at least once.

Statistical analysis supports our multivariate risk perception model and its associated hypotheses (Fig. 3.1). Indicators of national context, political attitudes and socio-economic status each have a significant effect on the perception of risks after controlling for the effect of other influences (Table 4.2). However, the impacts are not equal. Since all indicators are coded on the same scale, we can compare the marginal effect of significant indicators for each of the four groups to identify which has the most and the least impact.

The economic conditions of individuals and countries have the most influence on the extent to which people see the global economy as a big risk. Being satisfied with the national economy has the biggest marginal effect (-0.732), encouraging people to lower their perception of a global economic threat. Seeing oneself as being high in income has the second-biggest marginal effect (-0.259), and it likewise reduces the perception of economic risks. The greater influence of the evaluation of the national economy rather than the household economy is consistent with sociotropic theories that people evaluate national politics in the light of national circumstances. However, since the economically satisfied are a small fraction of Europeans, their total influence on perception of economic risk is limited, leaving the overall European concern with threats from the global economy high (see Table 4.1).

Even though most independent variables have a statistically significant effect on the perception of military threats, the scale of their marginal effect is less. The biggest individual-level effect, national sovereignty, is less than one-third the marginal effect of economic satisfaction on perceptions of the global economy. Moreover, the three indicators of nationalist attitudes have a combined effect on the perception of military risk that is a quarter less than that of economic satisfaction on views of the global economy. Distance from Moscow has the biggest marginal effect on views of military action, and its effect is almost double that of GDP per capita on the threat of the global economy.

Although valuing democracy is about an ideal concept rather than economic conditions, it has the biggest impact on perceptions of climate change. Moreover, it appears to be part of a cluster of influences associated with the rejection of nationalist views of sovereignty and immigration and being on the political left (Table 4.2). Moreover, the marginal effect of these influences on the perception of climate change is greater than the marginal effect of significant influences on military risks. This suggests there is a left-of-centre cluster of climate activists in Europe while there is nothing analogous promoting concern with military threats.

Notwithstanding the above differences, there is a widespread awareness among Europeans of threats to national security from the global economy, military action and climate change. This leaves open whether Europeans want their government to respond to security threats by going it alone or working with allies.

References

Converse, Philip E., 1964. 'The Nature of Belief Systems in Mass Publics'. In David Apter, ed., *Ideology and Discontent*, 206–261. New York: Free Press.

Kinder, Donald R. and Kiewiet, D. Roderick, 1981. 'Sociotropic Voting: The American Case', *British Journal of Political Science*, 11, 129–161.

Lockerbie, Brad, 2006. 'Economics and Politics: Egocentric or Sociotropic?', *American*, 27, Fall, 191–208.

Mudde, Cas, ed., 2016. *The Populist Radical Right: A Reader*. Abingdon: Routledge.

CHAPTER 5

Who Wants Which Allies?

Abstract National governments of Europe have always had allies they could look to for support when faced with threats to their national security. Today every European state belongs to dozens of multi-national organisations that differ in their purposes and in what they can add to the effectiveness of a national government acting on its own. Informal alliances such as the special relationship of Britain with the United States lack an institutional framework, but can still facilitate co-operation on security services. Democratic European governments need popular support to meet the costs that belonging to an alliance imposes. Whereas the government of the day's choice of allies commits all of its citizens, public opinion differs about whether allies are desirable in principle and if so, which ally would be best for dealing with a particular security threat: the EU, NATO or the UN. While there is majority support for defending security through alliances, Europeans do not rely on a single ally but pragmatically switch preferences between allies as the security threat changes.

Keywords Security · Allies · EU · NATO · UN · Isolation · Defence · Opinion · Climate change

© The Author(s), under exclusive license to Springer Nature Switzerland AG 2025
B. Weßels and R. Rose, *European Public Opinion about Security*, Palgrave Studies in European Union Politics, https://doi.org/10.1007/978-3-031-86263-2_5

National governments of Europe have always had allies they could look to for support when faced with threats to their national security. Sometimes alliances were due to marriage ties between ruling families, and sometimes they were based on religion. Today, every European state belongs to dozens of multi-national organisations nominally concerned with a great variety of issues. Informal alliances such as the special relationship of Britain with the United States lack an institutional framework, but can still facilitate co-operation between security services.

Security alliances differ in the breadth of their purposes, in the obligations and benefits of membership, and in what they can add to the effectiveness of a national government acting on its own. The European Union is strongest in economic policy and can affect national climate policies, but weak in defence due to a lack of a military force. The United Nations has broad purposes but cannot obligate its member governments to act on UN pronouncements. NATO is distinctive in being focused on a single purpose, the military defence of member states; in having a substantial armed force to give effect to this purpose; and in the obligation its treaty places on each member state, including the United States, to come to the defence of another member state if it is attacked.

Democratic governments need popular support to meet the costs that an alliance imposes on their freedom of choice in dealing with security issues. Gone are the days when foreign policy was regarded as a preserve of European aristocrats or technocrats. Nor can policymakers rely on the passive support of subjects lacking any opinion about security institutions. In the EuroSec survey, 96% expressed an opinion when asked about their government turning to an alliance for help with a specific security threat.

Whereas the government of the day's choice of allies commits all of its citizens, public opinion everywhere differs about whether allies are desirable in principle and, if so, which ally would be best for dealing with a particular security threat. This chapter starts by examining how much support there is among Europeans for their national government going it alone in dealing with security threats and whether those who favour going it alone are more likely to hold nationalist attitudes. The following section analyses how Europeans who favour allies differ from each other in which ally—the EU, NATO or the UN—they see as most helpful in dealing with security threats. While there is support for defending security through alliances, Europeans do not rely on a single ally but pragmatically switch preferences as the security threat changes.

5.1 Going It Alone

National leaders take an oath of office to defend their state. They do not take an oath of allegiance to the European Union or the United Nations; they sign a treaty setting out the scope of the institution's powers and, by omission, the powers they lack. When leaders of national governments meet in an alliance, the starting point of each is its national interest. The objective of discussions is to see how far these interests can be served by alliance policies.

The Default Position. Since the protection of national security is a defining responsibility of a modern state, when a security challenge arises, its government must respond. Its words may be forceful in an attempt to influence others, or vague, in order to mask its own indecisiveness or weakness. A statement by the prime minister or foreign secretary can offer assurance to citizens that it is protecting their security. Normally its diplomats will take soundings about the views of national allies, including the United States and the European Commission in Brussels. Diplomatic language leaves open the possibility of acting with allies, but is not a commitment to do so. Nor can a multi-national organisation obligate its members to act without national assent. The default position when a security problem arises is for a national government to consult with allies while leaving open what it decides to do on its own.

The majority of European governments belong to multiple alliances in which they can seek to advance their national interests through bargaining. For a national government to move beyond discussion with like-minded governments to acting as part of an alliance, it must believe that doing so will add enough effectiveness to compensate for the constraints being in an alliance places on acting on its own. A paradigm example of such a calculation has been governments giving up their national currency and empowering the European Central Bank (ECB) to replace it with the euro. Countries with a currency vulnerable to the international economy did so to gain greater currency stability and easier access to foreign finance. Germany gained the benefit of trading in a currency less likely to price German products out of international trade. Sweden has kept its national currency in order to manage the krona to protect full employment rather than accept the ECB's anti-inflation priority.

National governments have a political incentive for acting as part of an alliance. It multiplies the resources that can be used to advance a shared goal. In an effort to stop Russian aggression, national governments, singly and through the European Union, are sending aid to Ukraine to support what they see as a proxy war in their own defence. Collectively, the amount of aid is comparable with that of the United States and far greater than even the largest national donors, Germany and the United Kingdom, could supply on their own.

To test the extent to which there is unity in public opinion about their national government working in alliances, the EuroSec survey asked all respondents who saw a big or fair security risk whether they favoured their country going it alone in dealing with threats or getting help from a list of allies. Unlike the Eurobarometer survey, which only asks whether people endorse a single ally, the European Union, it offered a choice of four different allies or going it alone. Each potential ally could be considered effective in dealing with at least one type of risk. The European Union offers protection from the global economy as well as promoting a single European market; NATO and the United States provide collective military defence; and the United Nations deals with climate change. To avoid creating ephemeral answers (Converse 1964), respondents who saw little or no risk were not asked about going it alone or a choice of alliances.

The extent to which Europeans want to deal with security threats on their own differs from one type of risk to another (Fig. 5.1). A total of 46% favour their national government dealing with the global economy unconstrained by allies. This is consistent with the democratic principle of electoral accountability and the practice of parties competing for votes by emphasising economic issues.

Climate change is often described as a global problem due to pollution being transmitted across national boundaries and continents by air and water. Thus, the total amount of pollution affecting a country's climate is much greater than what it produces on its own. Cross-border pollution is particularly relevant in the many countries in close proximity to each other in Europe. Nonetheless, 38% of Europeans would prefer their government going it alone in dealing with the threat of climate change rather than relying on an alliance to deal with this global problem.

When military security is the issue, effectiveness takes priority. Deterring or repelling an aggressor requires a large army, and the population of Russia is far greater than the population of any European country. A big majority of Europeans appear aware of this; only 22% of EuroSec respondents think their country should go it alone in military defence.

5 WHO WANTS WHICH ALLIES? 59

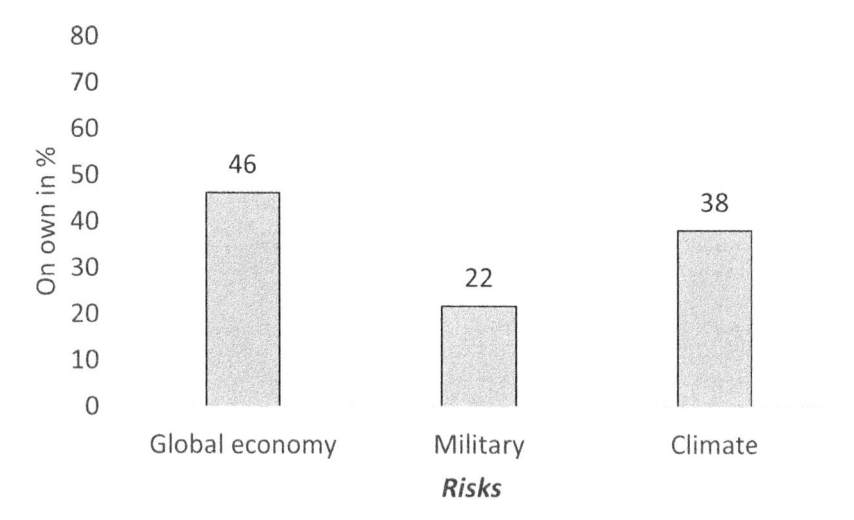

```
On own in %

80
70
60
50   46
40            38
30      22
20
10
 0
   Global economy  Military  Climate
              Risks
```

Fig. 5.1 Support for going it alone in security

Who Favours Going It Alone? Since going it alone is a strategy applicable across all forms of security, Hypothesis 3 suggests that the influences on going it alone should be much the same in the three regression analyses reported in Table 5.1.

Holding nationalist views ought to be specially important for avoiding alliances, since nationalism rejects foreign institutions on principle. This is the case. Giving priority to national sovereignty has the greatest marginal effect of any independent variable on going it alone in dealing with the global economy and military actions and a substantial effect on climate change. Endorsing the national government protecting the economy against foreign competition substantially boosts support for going it alone when dealing with the global economy and with climate change. Although immigration is an important issue in Europe and the EuroSec question explicitly referred to immigrants 'endangering the country's society by bringing new ideas and cultures', it did not have any significant influence on the materialist problems examined here.

Democracy is about arriving at a decision by a process of free deliberation with others before reaching a decision. It thus implies the rejection of going it alone in favour of working with allies. Viewing democracy as important positively encourages people to look for allies rather than

Table 5.1 Influences on going it alone in national security

	Economy (coeff.)	Military (coeff.)	Ecology (coeff.)
Democracy important	−0.689***	−1.237***	−0.263
Left_right	0.718	0.245	0.453
Immigration danger	0.200	0.525	0.129
National sovereignty	1.456***	1.216***	0.462***
Protection from imports	0.641***	0.406	0.830***
Strength of risk	−0.020	0.250	−0.141
Living standard	−0.822***	−0.699	−0.550
Positive nat'l economy	−0.810	−0.412	−0.511
Education	−0.157	−0.233	−0.333
Political interest	−0.198	0.108	−0.298***
Young (under 30)	−0.285	−0.178	−0.233***
Older (over 64)	−0.069	−0.263	−0.067
GDP per cap. PPP $	0.212		
Distance capital to Moscow		0.417	
Global warming 2022			−0.272
Intercept	−0.392	−2.196***	0.100
Number of observations	6180	3242	5541
Pseudo R^2	0.103	0.079	0.049

*** $p < 0.001$, * $p < 0.050$ Multi-level logistic regression
Independent variables normalised (0 minimum, 1 maximum)
Source European Security Survey, 2022

going it alone in dealing with the global economy and military defence. Moreover, the marginal effect of valuing democracy is large (Table 5.1). This rejects Robert Dahl's theory (1989: 319f) that membership in multi-national alliances will weaken popular commitment to democratic institutions.

People who identify strongly with a right-wing ideology, which is associated with populism, are significantly more likely to favour going it alone in handling the global economy and climate change. A concern with effective military defence makes NATO an acceptable alliance to Europeans of all kinds of ideological orientations. In a complementary manner, being on the left encourages support for working with allies to deal with problems of the global economy and climate change. However, the effect of a partisan ideology is less than half that of nationalist values.

The strength of security risks significantly affects attitudes towards alliances (Table 5.1). Europeans who see a strong risk rather than a fair risk to their military and climate change security are significantly more likely to want help from an alliance. When people see only a fair degree of risk, they are more likely to be prepared to view an alliance as unnecessary and accept their country going it alone.

Among socio-economic measures, it is an individual's view of their national economy rather than their living standard that is significant. People who are less satisfied with their country's national economy are more likely to favour going it alone in dealing with the global economy and climate change. This is consistent with politicians placing the blame for national economic problems on foreign influences. The impact is substantial albeit overshadowed by the much larger impact of nationalist values. By contrast, an individual's own standard of living, whether higher or lower within their society, has no significant effect on favouring going it alone or working within an alliance.

Whatever boost education may give to an understanding of international relations, it has no significant influence on favouring going it alone in dealing with the global economy or military defence. It does have a significant but limited impact on working with allies to deal with climate change. Having an interest in politics similarly gives significant but limited reinforcement to an individual preferring to work with allies to deal with climate change. The effect of age is also limited. Europeans under the age of 30 are significantly more likely to reject going it alone in favour of working with allies to deal with the global economy but the size of the impact is limited. Neither youth nor old age has a significant influence on going it alone for military action or climate change.

Differences in national resources do not affect whether citizens want their government to go it alone or seek an ally. All three indicators of national context fail to have a significant effect on popular support for going it alone (Table 5.1). A country's larger gross domestic product per capita does not encourage the mass of its population to favour going it alone. Nor does a country's proximity to Moscow have a significant effect on people wanting allies in dealing with military aggression. Likewise, the extent to which a country's climate has been warming fails to have a significant influence on going it alone or on individual attitudes towards climate change.

The analysis refines Hypothesis 2 by showing that political attitudes rather than socio-economic status have the most effect on whether Europeans want to go it alone or work with allies (Table 5.1). It also refines the hypothesis by showing that specific influences are important in different ways. For example, nationalist values associated with populist parties favour going it alone while valuing a liberal democracy has the opposite effect, favouring working with allies. Equally important, it rejects Hypothesis 1, since none of the three measures of national context has a significant effect on going it alone.

The majority of Europeans prefer working with allies to protect their security rather than going it alone in an insecure world. Although some significant variables such as left/right and nationalist/internationalist values divide Europeans, this is not evidence of American-style polarisation or, for that matter, polarisation as it is found in Poland. Individual attitudes are often selective, sometimes favouring going it alone and sometimes favouring an alliance. The median EuroSec respondent favours going it alone to deal with one security risk and twice working with allies. Among EuroSec respondents who take a consistent view, 40% favour alliances as against 15% consistently endorsing going it alone. In short, there is substantial support for maintaining alliances built up after the war to promote military and economic security and subsequently to protect the climate too.

5.2 Diversified Support for Diverse Allies

European governments have made decisions to join multiple alliances before most of their citizens were born, and sometimes before their current head of government was born. Among the eight countries in the European Security Survey, all were members of the United Nations by 1955. Two were founder members of NATO in 1949, and after the Berlin Wall fell all became members. Two EuroSec countries were founder members of the European Economic Community in 1957, half were members by 1995, and all the states but the United Kingdom are EU members today.

Just because a national government belongs to a formal alliance does not mean that it primarily relies on such a body to meet security threats. The contrary is often the case. Many organisations are diplomatic talking shops, where a government can show its face, call attention to its views and learn what other governments may share without a commitment to collective action.

The signals that European governments send their citizens about working in an alliance vary with the political priorities of the party in power. For example, the Polish government has shifted between being in the hands of a pro-EU coalition and a nationalist coalition challenging the EU's authority. Hungary has been governed by an anti-EU prime minister, Viktor Orban, since 2010. The signals also differ with the security situation. Until the Russian invasion of Ukraine, most governments saw the European Union as an economic community.

A majority of Europeans want an alliance to help defend their national security; however, the size of the majority differs depending on the issue at hand (Table 5.2). The only alliance endorsed by a majority of respondents is NATO, a single-purpose institution adding effectiveness to the military force of each member state (Table 5.2). Even though national governments recognise the United States as the dominant force in NATO, it was not endorsed in its own name by even one-tenth of Europeans. This shows that Europeans prefer to see NATO as a transatlantic alliance rather than having their national defence provided by the United States.

The European Union sees itself as a multi-purpose institution. However, only a minority of EU citizens who see security threats look to the EU for help in dealing with the global economy; less than one-third see it as the primary ally for climate change; and only one-tenth see the EU as offering major help in maintaining military security. The United Nations, another multi-purpose alliance, is even less likely to come first in the minds of Europeans. It is valued by one-quarter for what it can do to protect against climate change but its lack of effective powers results in it being almost completely ignored as a major ally for dealing with the global economy and military threats.

Table 5.2 Choice of ally differs by security threat

Q. *Which of the following can help our country deal with problems in the global economy? Military action? Climate change? Select one: the European Union, the United Nations, NATO, the United States, or our country must be able to look after itself on its own*

	Alliance favoured				
	EU	NATO	USA	UN	Any ally
	(As % of all respondents)				
Global economy	39	7	4	4	54
Climate change	31	4	2	24	62
Military threats	10	55	9	4	78

Source European Security Survey 2022

The European Union: Limited Public Support for Multi-Purpose Aspirations. The founders of European institutions had the overarching ambition of establishing a trio of institutions to maintain economic and military security. While this initial ambition was frustrated in the 1950s, the 1992 Maastricht Treaty gave it fresh life by rebranding the European Economic Community as the European Union with broad responsibilities in foreign affairs and defence.

By virtue of their national citizenship, all EuroSec respondents except Britons are European Union citizens too. However, they gave limited endorsement to their national government turning to the EU for help in dealing with security threats. Consistently, more people say they would prefer their country going it alone than working with the EU (cf. Tables 5.1 and 5.2). However, among those who favour working with an ally to deal with the global economy, the EU is endorsed by five to nine times as many people as any other institution.

Climate change was not an issue when the European Coal and Steel Community was founded in 1951; its purpose was to promote industrial development as well as prevent a strong German industry from once again serving a warring German military. The Maastricht Treaty described promoting environmental protection as one of the EU's many purposes. This was logical, since many environmental threats cross national boundaries that the EU has the power to regulate. The EU was named as the most favoured ally for dealing with climate change, albeit by a lower percentage than those wanting their government to go it alone in dealing with the climate.

The war in Ukraine has prompted EU institutions to co-ordinate financial and humanitarian assistance provided to Ukraine by member states as well as the EU budget (IfW Kiel 2024). It has opened up the option for the EU to make an important contribution to reconstructing Ukraine once the fighting stops (Rose 2025: chapter 9). However, helpful as such assistance is in economic terms, the EU lacks a military force of its own to deter military aggression. Europeans are well aware of this shortcoming. Only 10% of respondents see Brussels as the primary source of help in maintaining their own country's military security.

To identify influences on endorsing the EU as an ally as against other alternatives, we conducted a pair of regression analyses dividing respondents between those supporting the EU and those choosing another ally for dealing with the global economy and climate change. These analyses complement the regressions in Table 5.1 about those favouring going it alone. Since few respondents cited the EU as their favoured ally for military action, no further analysis was conducted of that alternative.

The EU's power to protect member states from the global economy divides Europeans according to their political attitudes (Table 5.3). Nationalists who want to protect their country's sovereignty and dislike immigrants changing their traditional national culture are substantially less likely to want the EU to act on their country's behalf in the international economy. In addition, people who see themselves on the right politically are also substantially less likely to favour the EU as an economic ally. Notwithstanding the EU's democratic deficit, people who value democracy highly are strongly in favour of allying with the EU in economic affairs after controlling for all other variables. The marginal effect is the largest of any significant variable.

Even though the EU is primarily an economic community, the socio-economic status of people who are EU citizens has no significant effect on their choice of an economic ally, whether the indicator is income level, satisfaction with the country's economic performance or education. The EU is not the sole choice of Europeans as a climate change ally. For every four EuroSec respondents who turn to the EU, three turn to the United Nations (Table 5.2).This suggests that support for the EU's economic activities is now so widespread that it is not a source of division along social structure lines. Notwithstanding the expression of different opinions by national governments at the EU's European Council, the primary division among European citizens on economic security is not so much between countries as between citizens within countries.

The United Nations: Multiple Purposes but No Clout. The UN was founded to reduce the risk of another world war; protection against climate change came later. Its chief asset is its global membership; this gives it the potential for global influence. National governments can use the UN as a platform for voicing their insecurities and calling for action to deal with collective security problems. This is also its chief liability, for its global membership reflects conflicting views about security in the world today. European governments have limited influence on the UN's agenda. They constitute less than one-fifth of the UN's membership, and their citizens are less than one-tenth of the world's population. The EU only has observer status at the UN.

Europeans are well aware of the UN's lack of resources to act effectively in response to global economic threats and military aggression. Only 4% see it as helpful to their country in dealing with the global

Table 5.3 Influences on wanting EU as economic ally

	Endorse EU as ally (coeff.)
Democracy important	1.649***
Left_Right	−0.628
Immigration danger	−0.687***
National sovereignty	−1.004***
Protection from imports	−0.232
Strength of risk	−0.245
Living standard	0.010
Positive nat'l economy	0.022
Education	0.174
Political interest	−0.015
Young (under 30)	−0.301
Older (over 64)	0.297
GDP per cap. PPP $	−1.055*
Intercept	2.118***
Number of observations	6180
Pseudo R^2	0.103

*** $p < 0.001$, * $p < 0.05$. Multi-level logistic regression
Independent variables normalised (0 minimum, 1 maximum)
Source European Security Survey, 2022

economy, and the same percentage see it as useful in deterring military aggression (Table 5.2). However, when it comes to protection against global climate change, the reach of the UN's membership gives it an advantage the EU lacks. Almost one-quarter of Europeans recognise this, seeing it as the best ally for promoting their climate security.

A regression analysis designed to identify Europeans who value the UN as the most suitable climate ally finds that they hardly differ from those who look for help to the EU or other alliances. None of the 13 independent variables has a statistically significant influence on wanting the UN as an ally in dealing with climate change. This result is virtually the same for a regression focused on having the EU as a climate change ally. Only one variable is significant, how strong the perception is of climate change as a risk (Table 5.4). The big division among Europeans is not about which institution they think would help most in dealing with climate change. It is between those who want their country to have an ally in dealing with global climate change and those who want to go it alone (Fig. 5.1).

NATO: High and Widespread Support for a North Atlantic Alliance. In a European setting NATO appears an anomaly: it places primary responsibility for European security outside Europe. This is because the United States is a superpower with a bigger and better-equipped military force than any European state. It can thus be a more effective deterrent to Russian aggression than the military force that any European state can muster on its own. As long as the United States government sees deterring Russian military action as in the American national interest, NATO fills the void created by the European Union's lack of an effective armed force of its own. At the time of the European Security survey, President Joseph Biden's administration was committed to NATO.

NATO is endorsed as a desirable ally by a majority of Europeans. A total of 55% of Europeans who see military action as a substantial threat to their country want it as an ally. By contrast, in the United States opinion about NATO now tends to be divided along partisan lines (see Sect. 6.2). European endorsement of NATO is 31 percentage points higher than that for the United Nations as an ally in dealing with climate change and 16 percentage points higher than the EU for the economy (Table 5.2).

Widespread popular endorsement of NATO means that a regression analysis finds no polarisation of European opinion along political or socio-economic lines. There is no significant statistical difference in support for NATO among those on the right and the left or those with a higher and a lower economic status. Only one of the thirteen independent variables

Table 5.4 Influences on wanting UN or EU as climate change ally

	Endorse as climate ally	
	UN (coeff.)	EU (coeff.)
Democracy important	0.228	0.557
Left_Right	−0.075	−0.013
Immigration danger	−0.082	−0.039
National sovereignty	0.215	−0.387
Protection from imports	−0.068	−0.072
Strength of risk	0.074	−0.136***
Living standard	−0.251	0.246
Positive nat'l economy	0.452	−0.373
Education	0.342	−0.191
Political interest	−0.015	−0.032
Young (under 30)	−0.146	−0.067
Older (over 64)	0.065	0.092
Global warming 2022	−0.684	0.736
Intercept	−0.757	0.031
Number of observations	3,538	3,538
Pseudo R^2	0.014	0.019

*** $p < 0.001$, * $p < 0.05$. Multi-level logistic regression
Independent variables normalised (0 minimum, 1 maximum)
Source European Security Survey, 2022

is statistically significant. Believing that democracy is important gives a substantial boost to supporting NATO (Table 5.5).

The EuroSec survey offered the United States as well as NATO as a possible ally. A total of 9% endorsed having the United States an ally. The proportion choosing the United States was as high as 20% in Poland and 14% in Britain, but down to 5% in Germany. However, there were no significant independent variables. The widespread support for NATO and the United States among EuroSec respondents, including people who see themselves on the left and right, stands in contrast with the United States, where public opinion about military security has become polarised along partisan lines during the presidency of Donald Trump.

Public Opinion About Alliances Varies. Even though opinion polls show widespread popular distrust of national governments (Sasaki 2019), Europeans expect their national government to act when national security is threatened. However, there is no agreement about whether the government should act on its own or as part of an alliance. Differences

Table 5.5 Influences on wanting a military ally

	Endorse as military ally	
	NATO (coeff.)	USA (coeff.)
Democracy important	0.979***	−0.292
Left_Right	0.338	0.426
Immigration danger	−0.400	0.816
National sovereignty	−0.062	−0.096
Protection from imports	0.305	−0.333
Strength of risk	−0.245	0.384
Living standard	−0.388	0.140
Positive nat'l economy	−0.360	0.257
Education	0.402	−0.166
Political interest	−0.263	0.407
Young (under 30)	−0.281	0.169
Older (over 64)	0.158	−0.051
Distance capital to Moscow	−0.828	0.203
Intercept	1.295*	−3.911***
Number of observations	2,563	2563
R^2 for overall model	0.035	0.025

*** $p < 0.001$, * $p < 0.05$. Multi-level logistic regression
Independent variables normalised (0 minimum, 1 maximum)
Source European Security Survey, 2022

about policy choices are normal in a democracy, and national security is no exception. Elites can disagree with each other about security, as is evident in Berlin and Washington today. The EuroSec survey shows that the mass of Europeans disagree with each other too.

Many Europeans are subject to cross-pressures when asked to make security choices, holding political attitudes that push in opposite directions. Among respondents who give a high priority to protecting national sovereignty, which encourages support for going it alone, 76% also place a very high value on living in a democracy, which favours working in an alliance. Among those who give a very high value to living in a democracy, 34% are subject to cross-pressures because they also want to protect national sovereignty.

Cross-pressures can lead individuals to varying in their view of allies depending on the specific security threat. Among those who favour working with the European Union to deal with the global economy, more than two-thirds prefer working with NATO to deal with military threats and one-third prefer dealing with climate change by working with other allies. Even though the European Union today claims the authority to deal with all three types of security threats, only 5% who see fair or big security threats make the European Union their first choice as an ally in dealing with all three threats. In other words, the Maastricht Treaty's assignment of responsibility for foreign affairs and security policy to Brussels is an example of European overreach rather than European integration.

Europeans are not polarised in their overall view of security. The views of 44% of EuroSec respondents about alliances or going it alone varied; they sometimes endorsed working within an alliance and sometimes favoured going it alone. Even among those who wanted an ally for dealing with all three risks, the great majority differed in their choice of ally according to type of threat. Instead of being subject to cognitive dissonance by holding contrasting views, most Europeans appear to make discriminating judgements about the effectiveness of potential allies or going it alone. A high level of education is not required for individuals to see that the European Union, the source of the currency that most Europeans hold in their pocket, has economic clout. Nor does one need to watch war movies to know that their country's armed force is no match for a superpower.

Policymakers can make use of the openness of citizens to alternative allies depending on what is effective in a given situation. For example, if climate change causes a flood in a national river, then the national government can provide flood protection. However, if the flood originates upstream in another EU country, then the national government must work with allies to protect its citizens from flooding. Cross-pressures can be invoked to modify the opinion of those who favour national sovereignty by selectively emphasising common values. For example, NATO can be justified as protecting European democracies from a heavily armed authoritarian aggressor, the Soviet Union.

European governments can also look for passive support from those who are unconcerned, having no opinion or seeing little or no threat from a particular form of security. When asked about the risk of military action, 51% had no opinion or saw little or no risk to their country in the early months of the war in Ukraine. Similarly, 20% are unconcerned about climate change and 12% about a fair or big risk from the global economy. When protecting national security requires imposing costs on European citizens, as has become NATO policy in the light of developments in Moscow and Washington, a democratic government can try to use an increased threat to mobilise support for its policy by increasing the awareness of military threats among that section of its population that had previously taken their security for granted.

The thinking of Europeans today appears consistent with the pragmatic philosophy of Jean Monnet: people support different alliances to deal with different kinds of threats. In doing so they are not denying that their own country lacks resources to act on its own, but recognising limits on its national capacity to provide security in a globalising world. The geographical coverage of each alliance is also pragmatic. They differ in their 'Europeanness', since threats to security are not confined to states that belong to the European Union. NATO bridges two continents, depending for its effectiveness on the United States government continuing to regard defending Europe as in America's national interest. The United Nations has the global reach to deal with global climate change, much of it caused by populous countries beyond Europe. The European Union offers members protection against tariff and non-tariff barriers that can be imposed by major countries in the global economy such as the United States. The complicated structure of security alliances is not a rejection of European integration (cf. Stubb 1996). It is a strategy of differentiated policy integration: effectiveness in dealing with a particular security threat is more important than whether it advances the cause of European integration for its own sake.

References

Converse, Philip E., 1964. 'The Nature of Belief Systems in Mass Publics'. In David Apter, ed., *Ideology and Discontent*, 209–261. New York: Free Press.

Dahl, Robert A., 1989. *Democracy and Its Critics*. New Haven: Yale University Press.

IfW Kiel, 2024. *The Ukraine Tracker*. Kiel: Institute for the World Economy, www.ifw-kiel.de/topics/war-against-ukraine/ukraine-support-tracker/.

Rose, Richard, 2025. *European Security from Ukraine to Washington*. London: Bloomsbury.

Sasaki, Masamichi, ed., 2019. *Trust in Contemporary Society*. Leiden: Brill.

Stubb, Alexander, 1996. 'A Categorization of Differentiated Integration', *Journal of Common Market Studies*, 34, 2, 283–295.

CHAPTER 6

Europeans Pragmatic About Security

Abstract There is little that individuals can do to protect themselves from negative developments in the global economy, military action and climate change. They see their government as sometimes being able to act on its own and sometimes needing to act in an alliance with other governments in order to gain effectiveness. The choice of allies—the EU, NATO or the UN—is pragmatic. The selection of a particular multi-national institution as an ally does not reflect a common identity or shared values. Nor is it the expression of a desire to advance European integration or world government. Instead, it reflects a self-interested calculation that a particular alliance has the resources to protect a country's security more effectively than a national government could do on its own. Europeans show their pragmatic recognition of these differences by sometimes favouring one ally, sometimes another and sometimes wanting their country to go it alone. Since challenges to security change over time, the chapter's conclusion marshals empirical data to show the extent to which pressures from events and long-term trends have altered or left relatively stable European attitudes towards security since the Russian invasion of Ukraine.

Keywords Security · Threats · Allies · Opinion · Defence · European Union · NATO · UN · Climate

© The Author(s), under exclusive license to Springer Nature Switzerland AG 2025
B. Weßels and R. Rose, *European Public Opinion about Security*, Palgrave Studies in European Union Politics,
https://doi.org/10.1007/978-3-031-86263-2_6

Europeans are anxious about their security. Many see substantial threats from the global economy, military action and climate change. Since there is little that individuals can do to protect themselves, they look to their government to do something to help them. Chapter 5 shows that, while Europeans place a high value on living in a democracy in which their governors are accountable, they also have a pragmatic view about what their government can and cannot do to protect their security. People sometimes see it as being able to act on its own and sometimes needing to act in an alliance with other governments in order to be effective.

The choice of allies is pragmatic. Selecting a particular multi-national institution as an ally need not reflect a common identity or shared values or a desire to advance European integration or world government as an end in itself. Instead, it reflects a self-interested calculation that a particular alliance has the resources to protect a country's security more effectively than a national government could do on its own.

Politicians want to gain votes by promising to deliver peace and prosperity more effectively than their competitors. However, if they are successful in winning office, this creates a new challenge: voters will hold them accountable for delivering what they promise. The consequences of failure are readily apparent to voters: rising prices, a deteriorating climate, or menacing actions by drones or armed forces. Only if the government is effective in delivering what it promises will it appear credible when seeking re-election.

Politicians thus have a pragmatic incentive to make promises about security that are effective as well as popular. However, when a threat comes from beyond rather than within its borders, the effectiveness of a policy is not entirely in a government's control. Threats to national security take place in an environment in which powerful and weak national governments and multi-national institutions interact along with non-state actors. Outcomes emerge rather than being determined by a single government. This places limits on the dialogue between parties and voters in which parties propose policies and citizens mandate parties to deliver what they promise.

Because the protection of national security is a functional problem, the next section sets out different ways in which multi-national institutions can protect the security of Europeans. Since challenges to security change over time, the chapter's conclusion marshals empirical evidence of the extent to which pressures to change have altered European attitudes towards security threats or left opinions relatively stable since the EuroSec survey was conducted.

6.1 Security Is About Effectiveness

Whereas states are defined by their boundaries, multi-national alliances are defined by their purposes. This creates a great variety of institutions that national governments can join, depending on their functional effectiveness. In dealing with their responsibilities for the economy and military defence, national governments have formed different alliances with different capacities and purposes.

The European Union's founders were pragmatic. Instead of campaigning for the remote ideal of a United States of Europe, they aimed to protect European security through three complementary institutions, each with a different function: a European Economic Community (EEC), a European Defence Community and a European Political Community. The French National Assembly torpedoed the European Defence Community treaty in 1954. This has resulted in European governments differentiating their allies. They rely on the European Union for economic resources, on NATO for military defence and on their own policies or the UN to deal with climate change.

The European Economic Community created by the Treaty of Rome in 1957 had the authority to promote trade among its six member states if there was a consensus. Its preamble ambitiously claimed that this would 'lay the foundations of an ever closer union among the peoples of Europe'. In the decades that have followed, the EEC has gradually expanded its functions to become the multi-purpose European Union. It has exclusive power over trade and the monetary policy of eurozone countries, transforming national markets into a single European market. It has also gained ancillary powers as spillover effects create a convenient justification for expanding Brussels' functions into social policy and foreign affairs (Rosamond 2000; cf. Sandholtz and Stone-Sweet 2012).

During its long life the EU has given priority to promoting trade by reducing or eliminating barriers to cross-border trade inherited from a mercantilist era. The European Central Bank (ECB) has replaced the national currencies of 20 countries with the multi-national euro. This removes currency fluctuations from the trade in goods and services from Finland and Slovakia to Spain and Ireland. Mediterranean countries that had weak currencies can now borrow more cheaply, and German businesses export goods at a more competitive price than if they were denominated in a strong Deutsche Mark.

The expansion of the European Union from 6 to 27 members has made the EU a significant actor in the global economy. The population of the single European market is larger than the United States, making it a target for foreign exporters, and creating European industries that are major international exporters. The EU has used its monopoly of trade powers to negotiate 42 agreements to promote trade with 74 countries. In 2023 the trade was valued at 2.3 trillion euros (https://policy.trade.ec.europa.eu/eu-trade-relationships-country-and-region/negotiations-and-agreements_en).

Embedding EU institutions in national economies has introduced path dependence as a new criterion for remaining a member. The cumulative effect of past commitments makes the cost of withdrawal so disruptive nationally that it would be too costly to leave (Pierson 2000). The Greek government's experience in the eurozone illustrates this. Initially, Greek membership brought economic benefits to the country by boosting public spending financed by borrowing money cheaply in euros. When this led to a financial crisis, the ECB demanded that Greece accept harsh financial conditions before it would re-finance the Greek government's debts. The Greek prime minister Alexis Tsipras claimed an electoral mandate to reject these terms and raised the prospect of Greece withdrawing from the eurozone. However, confronted with the likely impact on the Greek economy of withdrawing, Tsipras accepted the ECB's conditions rather than trigger the collapse of the country's finances.

As the United Kingdom was not a member of the eurozone, it could and did call a referendum on leaving the European Union. Proponents of withdrawal promised that taking back control of the United Kingdom's political economy would enable the British government to promote economic growth more effectively at no cost. In 2016 a majority voted for withdrawal. Economic analysis indicates that Brexit has had the opposite effect of its intent, hurting rather than helping British economic growth (UK Office for Budget Responsibility 2024). The United Kingdom's experience has been noted by populist parties declaring they want to take back control from Brussels. As the nationalist government of Hungary shows, Viktor Orban prefers to fight for more economic benefits within the EU rather than go it alone, as the United Kingdom has done.

As long as there is a consensus among EU member states, their policies can promote European integration. However, efforts by the European Commission to promote a single European foreign affairs and security policy have made little headway because of the lack of a consensus. The majority of EuroSec respondents pragmatically endorse differentiated integration to protect their security. The choice of an ally depends on the function. While almost two in five EuroSec respondents endorse turning to the EU for protection from the global economy, only one-tenth see the EU as a major ally for military security.

More Europeans endorse their national government acting on its own than relying on Brussels for climate change security (Table 5.2). The answer that Europeans give to the question 'Who can help protect our security?' is 'It depends on the problem at hand'.

NATO is the prime example of a multi-national institution reducing its functions to a narrow minimum—the military protection of the European territory of its member states. The national governments of Europe have prized NATO membership because it makes their military power far more effective by adding the United States' armed forces to what each country can muster by going it alone. For three-quarters of a century this has deterred Russia from attacking NATO's members.

Europeans prefer to see NATO as a military alliance of countries sharing a common interest rather than as an organisation in which the United States is the dominant force. When offered a choice between turning for help to NATO or the United States, by a margin of six to one EuroSec respondents choose NATO (Table 5.2). By contrast, national governments have quietly accepted the United States acting as NATO's hegemonic leader and relying on it to bear most of the financial cost of maintaining a formidable military force.

While the effectiveness of an American-led military force has been a constant, the political commitment of the United States to defend Europe has been called into question by the White House's response to Russia's invasion of Ukraine. President Joseph Biden regarded Russia's invasion as a threat to American national interest, and the United States has been the leading country in supplying Ukraine with military equipment. By contrast, President Donald Trump has repeatedly indicated that he does not regard the defence of Ukraine as vital to America's national security. Moreover, he has claimed that he could end the war in Ukraine promptly by negotiating a deal with President Vladimir Putin, albeit at Ukraine's expense. The Pew Research Center found in November 2024 that 42%

of Democrats view Russia's invasion of Ukraine as a threat to America's national interests compared to 19% of Republicans. Moreover, 41% of Republicans think the United States is providing too much aid to Ukraine compared to 13% of Democrats (Pew Research Center 2024).

To address *climate change*, governments must deal effectively with its causes, which operate across oceans and continents. There are limits to the effectiveness of actions by a national government, which can deal on its own with local pollution but not a continental climate. Actions by EU institutions can affect the European climate but have only a limited effect on global climate threats originating in the western hemisphere and in Asia. Logically, effective action requires co-ordinated action on a global scale.

Although the European Union developed well before climate change became a major issue, its economic powers give it a significant resource to regulate some causes of environmental harm. There are half a dozen directorates within the European Commission that can propose climate controls, and the European Climate Law calls for European countries to neutralise their impact on the environment by 2050. However, effective implementation is in the hands of national governments. Climate change policies must compete for government funds with social policies and impose costs on citizens' home heating and use of their automobile, thereby creating a pushback from voters, as the British and German governments have found.

The United Nations has promoted awareness of the measures needed to combat climate change through a Framework Convention. It holds periodic global conferences to review and debate progress in protecting the environment (https://unfccc.int/). However, it lacks the power to act effectively on its own. The implementation of its recommendations depends on the voluntary action of its member states. These include the world's major polluters as well as the countries affected by a polluted climate. While the UN has the soft power to call the attention of governments to measures they could adopt to reduce climate change, it lacks the means to make its members act.

The attractiveness of an alliance is not always matched by its effectiveness. Because political judgements about the effectiveness of policies are subjective, national leaders can and do miscalculate the effects of joining an alliance. Benito Mussolini hesitated to commit Italy to the risk of becoming a military ally of Hitler's Germany when the Second World War started in September 1939. However, once France began falling to the German army the following spring, Mussolini entered the war and occupied parts of southern France and Libya. Five years later the effect of this decision was military defeat, the end of a fascist dictatorship and Mussolini's execution. By contrast, Generalissimo Francisco Franco resisted taking Spain into the Second World War in favour of a strategy of going it alone. Spain remained formally neutral, shifting with the fortunes of war from favouring the Axis to the Allied armies. Franco's regime survived until his death in 1975.

6.2 Pressures to Change

Keeping national security stable, particularly if there is peace, prosperity and an equable climate, is the ideal situation. However, this is easier said than done. National security systems are part of interdependent international systems subject to unexpected events and pressures from many sources. Threats can come from abroad, such as Russia's aggression in Ukraine. Within the European Union there can be resistance to change strengthened by major policy changes requiring the unanimous approval of its 27 diverse members. When pressures take decades to become evident, as is the case with climate change, the appearance of stability can persist before there is a visible effect on public opinion and policy.

Public opinion can respond to pressures on security in a variety of ways. Survey data is bound to show sampling fluctuations from year to year. If changes are of little or no significance, opinion will be completely stable. If there are significant pressures up and down, as long as they cancel each other out in the course of time, then opinion remains in a dynamic equilibrium. A third alternative is a trend in which small annual changes in the same direction cumulatively produce a substantial long-term change. In Figs. 6.1 and 6.2 a least-squares regression line shows the extent to which year-to-year changes are fluctuations or show a steady positive or negative trend in attitudes towards the EU as an ally, as measured by the Eurobarometer survey. An unexpected event with a major impact on security can destabilise public opinion by abruptly giving it a boost or by showing a big reversal in what people think.

A critical question in this study is whether public opinion about security issues has remained the same. Since the European Security Survey was conducted in late autumn 2022. To ascertain this, for each security threat we show measures over time of influences on attitudes towards alliances and evidence about how public opinion reacts. In addition we take into

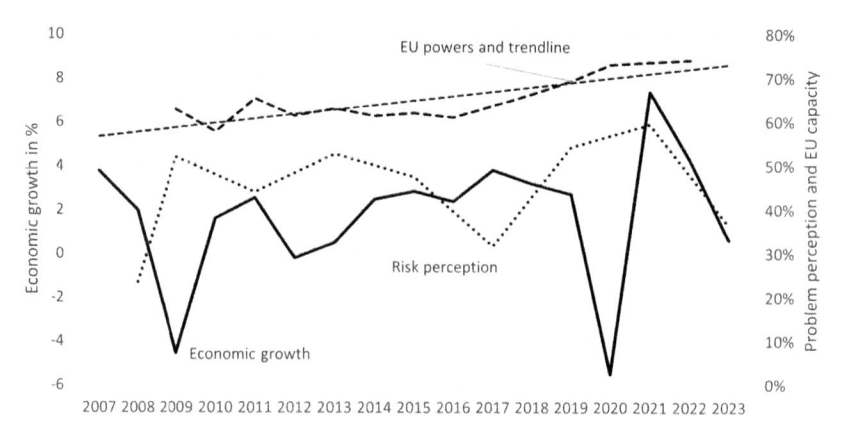

Fig. 6.1 Trend endorsement of EU as economic ally

account events that can shock perceptions of security, such as Russian aggression in Ukraine or COVID.

Economic Pressures. The economy is always in flux, whether the indicator is the rate of economic growth, inflation or unemployment. The publication of economic statistics quarterly or monthly means that fluctuations up and down, even if minuscule, can be headlined far more frequently than election results. Over a period of time, these movements create pressures that may affect the opinion of Europeans about the management of the global economy.

The year 2008 was the start of a shock economic recession triggered by an unexpected crisis in American financial markets. The economies of EuroSec countries contracted an average of 4.5 percentage points that year (Fig. 6.1). The prompt reaction of national governments and the European Central Bank resulted in a swift recovery the subsequent year. The years that followed were marked by fluctuating annual growth rates until the COVID pandemic prompted a drastic but temporary curtailment of economic activity. In consequence, there was a contraction of 5.5 percentage points in 2020, followed by an upswing of 7.3 percentage points the following year. Resilience regained all the economic ground lost under COVID.

Europeans have shown resilience in their reaction to economic fluctuations. When Eurobarometer surveys asked what people perceived as their country's four most important problems in 2009, a total of 52% named

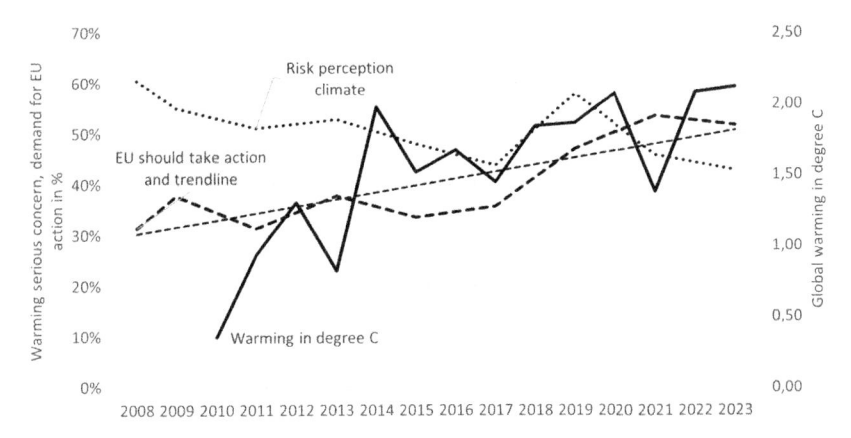

Fig. 6.2 Trend endorsement of EU helping with climate change

the economic situation. In the years that followed, the importance of the economy has fluctuated down and up (Fig. 6.1). It fell two years later only to rise again to 53% in 2013. The subsequent increase in growth reduced concern with the economy as a problem. The shock effect of COVID once again made the economy a serious concern for a majority of Europeans. Effective resilience has resulted in concern falling to 36% in 2023 as other issues such as the war in Ukraine gained attention.

Throughout the ups and downs in economic growth, national governments have accepted the European Union acting as an ally, and so have European citizens. To assess public opinion about the EU as an ally, the Eurobarometer asks whether people agree with the statement: *The EU has sufficient power and tools to defend the economic interests of Europe in the global economy.* Replies show continuing majority support for the EU as an economic ally. The proportion taking this view was 65% in early 2009 and 69% in spring 2023. Even though this trend cannot be applied directly to the EuroSec question about having the EU as an ally, its relative stability indicates that the EuroSec result about having the EU as an ally may also be considered stable.

The return to the White House of Donald Trump gives new significance to the EU's exclusive power to control the trade of its member states. The EU has been used to promote free trade abroad as well as free trade within the EU. The United States is the EU's biggest export market, accounting for one-fifth of its total export of goods and services, while the United States has had a $131 billion trade deficit with Europe. President Trump has described tariffs as a beautiful weapon to use against countries running a trade surplus with the United States. In his first term he placed selective tariffs on European manufacturers. After being inaugurated for a second term, President Trump placed a 20% tariff on goods manufactured in the European Union.

Climate Change. While the climate can change overnight, the change that most concerns policymakers—global warming—has taken many years to become politically significant. Temperature change from year to year is very gradual and can even go down rather than up from one year to the next. Nonetheless, from one decade to the next there has been a tendency for temperatures to rise cumulatively (Fig. 6.2). Between 2010 and 2023 the mean temperature in EuroSec countries increased by an average of 1.76 °C.

While every European is exposed to climate change, the climate alters at a much slower rate than economic conditions or military threats. Nonetheless, slow-moving changes in the climate combined with media statements by climate experts and demands by activists have established climate change as a major problem facing European countries. When the Eurobarometer asked about it in 2010, climate change was viewed as a serious threat by 55% of respondents. It has since fluctuated within a range between 43% and 58% in competition for public concern with such threats as COVID and the war in Ukraine.

European public opinion is increasingly aware of the need for national governments to seek help from international organisations to deal with rising temperatures. The Eurobarometer asks respondents to select institutions suitable for tackling climate change and offers a list of ten groups ranging from individuals to national governments and the European Union. When the question was asked in 2011, the EU was chosen by just 31% of respondents (Fig. 6.2). Since then there has been an underlying trend in support for the EU acting on climate change, amounting to a rise of 20 percentage points by 2023. Just as the COVID pandemic showed global health threats required a multi-national response, so more than half of Europeans now see the EU as helpful for dealing with climate change.

Pressures on Defence. Most European adults were born during the Cold War when the Soviet Union presented a military threat; its collapse greatly reduced the number of people who saw its successor, the Russian Federation, as a serious threat until after Vladimir Putin became president. He has taken steps to redress what he saw as a great tragedy, the dissolution of the Soviet Union. In 2008 Russian forces supported South Ossetia breaking away from the Republic of Georgia. In 2014 military action allowed Russia to annex Crimea and parts of eastern Ukraine.

Europeans have responded to shock military action in the near abroad. Whereas economic and climate change pressures have been persisting, the onset of military pressures has been abrupt. After Russia seized Crimea from Ukraine in 2014, the percentage of people in EuroSec countries seeing armed conflict as a serious threat jumped from 31% to 41%. Concern with military conflict then receded to 22% in 2021, but following the Russian invasion of Ukraine in February 2022 a total of 51% in EuroSec countries saw armed conflict as a serious threat.

Prior to the war in Ukraine the Public Diplomacy division of NATO began conducting public opinion surveys in member states about attitudes towards the NATO alliance. In reply to the question *How important do you consider the relationship between North America and Europe in dealing with security challenges today?*, 85% described ties as fairly or very important in 2019. While peace and war in Ukraine have fluctuated since, popular support for NATO in Europe has remained stable, showing no significant trend. Moreover, Public Diplomacy's spring 2024 survey found that if there were a referendum on NATO membership, more than five-sixths of respondents would vote for their country remaining a member of NATO.

American opinion about defending fellow NATO members has been polarising. A February 2025 survey found that while 81% of American Democrats had a favourable opinion of NATO, only 51% of Republicans did. Thus, overall American support for NATO is lower than among Europeans (Pew Research Center 2025; Tama and Friedrichs 2024).

Pragmatic Responses to Pressures. Europeans do not see threats to national security as always being at the same level, and the attention paid to security competes with domestic concerns on the political agenda, such as health care and managing the national debt. Europeans are also selective. They differ in giving priority to working with allies or going it alone, depending on the problem at hand and allies' effectiveness. People respond pragmatically to pressures created by the specific dynamics of the global economy, military action and climate change rather than making judgments according to general principles of co-operation or self-reliance.

Public opinion about the economy is resilient; it fluctuates up and down in keeping with movements in the national and international economies. When pressures heighten, more people see the global economy as a serious problem, and it does not recede much when economic pressures subside. The division in opinion about going it alone or relying on the EU to deal with the global economy is a statement of priorities in a multi-level economy in which both national governments and the EU have responsibilities. With dual national and European citizenship, people can use national elections to hold national policymakers accountable while looking to the EU to use its trade and monetary powers for protection from the global economy.

Awareness of the threat of climate change is promoted by global media coverage of green activists and expert evidence. There is also recognition that climate change is not a problem that can be handled by national governments on their own but requires co-operative action to be effective. There has been a 19 percentage point increase in public support for the EU playing a part in combating climate change and 55% of EuroSec respondents endorse either the EU or the UN as their first choice as an ally. This suggests popular support for the complementary development of European and global climate policies.

Europeans are ready to respond when military activities change from theoretical risks to near-at-hand threats. Serious public concern about military aggression rose 10 percentage points after Russia seized Crimea in 2014 and rose even more to 51% after Russian troops invaded Ukraine. The EuroSec survey shows that European citizens are not taken in by the attempts of European institutions to shoulder responsibility for military security when it lacks an effective armed force. The European public's support for NATO as a military ally is significantly higher than support for the EU as an ally in dealing with other types of security threats.

However, European public opinion has yet to adapt to political polarisation in the United States about whether defending Europe is in the American national interest. In an average of polls in EuroSec countries before the 2024 presidential election, 67% endorsed the Democratic candidate, Kamala Harris, against 33% saying they supported Donald Trump. There were wide differences between countries: only 10% of Swedes and 16% of Germans said they would vote for Trump, while 62% of Hungarians followed their leader, Viktor Orban, in endorsing Trump (https://europeelects.eu/2024/11/04/u-s-election-europeans-would-vote-for-harris-if-they-could/).

National governments have bitten their lips to congratulate the re-elected Donald Trump while privately describing Trump's victory as a threat to NATO and much else. If President Trump carries through his threat to impose tariffs on countries that run trade surpluses with the United States, this will have a direct impact on European economic growth. It would also have an indirect political effect, as any money that a government collected in retaliatory tariffs would likely be offset by tax revenue lost due to economic contraction. If the Trump administration chose, it could divide EU member states by imposing high tariffs on selected countries considered unfriendly such as Germany and no tariffs on countries considered friendly such as Hungary.

Whether or how President Trump follows through on his political threats, his America First rhetoric has already stimulated European governments to give up their assumption that they can rely on the unconditional commitment of American force in the event of Russian aggression against a European member state. Boosting defence expenditure may reassure Washington that Europe is willing to contribute more money to collective defence and should increase the capacity of European countries to act if Washington proves unwilling to maintain protection. In 2024 European defence expenditure finally reached the target of 2% of GDP, a one-third increase from when Donald Trump first entered the White House eight years ago. Poland and Estonia, frontline countries with Russia, now spend a bigger share of their GDP on defence than the United States.

Even before Donald Trump returned to the White House, there was talk of the need to increase European spending on defence to 3% or higher (The Economist 2024). Increasing public spending on defence will put pressure on government spending for popular domestic policies. It will require European governments to mobilise greater popular awareness of threats from Russian aggression and Washington's unreliability than was found in the 2022 European Security Survey.

European public opinion today reflects lessons that the founders of EU institutions learned from two wars spreading death and destruction across Europe in their lifetime. Many Europeans recognise that dealing effectively with threats to national security cannot be achieved solely by their own government. This has led national governments to create multi-national alliances to increase their capacity to defend their security effectively. As long as a threat to national security is perceived as substantial, our empirical evidence shows that a majority of Europeans are prepared to give up a degree of national sovereignty to make their country more secure in a world full of threats.

References

Pew Research Center, 2024. *Nato Seen Favourably in Member States*. Washington DC: . Pew Research Center.

Pew Research Center, 2025. *Americans' views of the war in Ukraine continue to differ by party*. Washington DC: Pew Research Centre.

Pierson, Paul, 2000. 'Increasing Returns, Path Dependence, and the Study of Politics', *American Political Science Review*, 94, 2, 251–267, https://doi.org/10.2307/2586011.

Rosamond, Ben, 2000. *Theories of European Integration*. New York: St Martin's Press.

Sandholtz, Wayne and Stone-Sweet, Alec, 2012. 'Neo-Functionalism and Supranational Governance'. In Erik Jones, Anand Menon and Stephen Weatherill, eds., *The Oxford Handbook of the European Union*, 18–33. Oxford: Oxford University Press.

Tama, Jordan and Friedrichs, Gordon M., 2024. *Polarization and US Foreign Policy: When Politics Crosses the Water's Edge*. London: Palgrave Macmillan.

The Economist, 2024. "NATO and America: Spend to Defend". London: *The Economist*, 30 November.

UK Office for Budget Responsibility, 2024. 'Brexit Analysis'. London, https://obr.uk/forecasts-in-depth/the-economy-forecast/brexit-analysis/.

Appendix: List of Variables

Variable, question number	N	Mean	Stan. dev.	Range
Strength of risk				
Global economy, Q30a	11,919	3.30	0.71	No risk to big 1–4
Military threats, Q30b	11,604	2.55	0.85	No risk to big 1–4
Climate change, Q30e	12,024	3.16	0.84	No risk to big 1–4
Number of perceived risks	11,297	2.17	0.84	Range 0–3
Allies to deal with security, Q31–Q34				
EU, economic ally	4802	0.73	0.44	EU = 1; all others = 0
NATO, military ally	3822	0.71	0.46	NATO = 1; all others = 0
UN, climate ally	4992	0.51	0.50	UN = 1; all others = 0
EU, climate ally	4992	0.39	0.49	EU = 1; all others = 0
On our own—economy	8952	0.46	0.50	1 = On own; 0 = Any ally
On our own—military	4892	0.22	0.41	1 = On own; 0 = Any ally
On our own—climate change	8077	0.38	0.49	1 = On own; 0 = Any ally
Political attitudes				
Democracy valued, Q17e	11,872	6.16	1.26	Not at all to high 0–10
Left/right scale, Q14	10,578	4.16	1.65	Left to right 1–7
Immigration endangers society, Q16f	10,467	3.81	2.11	1 disagree, 7 agree

(continued)

© The Editor(s) (if applicable) and The Author(s), under exclusive license to Springer Nature Switzerland AG 2025
B. Weßels and R. Rose, *European Public Opinion about Security*, Palgrave Studies in European Union Politics, https://doi.org/10.1007/978-3-031-86263-2

APPENDIX: LIST OF VARIABLES

(continued)

Variable, question number	N	Mean	Stan. dev.	Range
Sovereignty endangered, Q16g	9608	4.41	1.99	1 disagree, 7 agree
Protection from imports, Q16h	10,363	4.54	1.90	1 disagree, 7 agree
Socio-demographics				
Income standard, Q41	12,302	3.85	1.16	Poor to rich 1–7
Positive nat'l economy, Q24b	12,079	2.95	1.72	Negative to positive 1–7
Education, Q4	12,695	2.14	0.65	Low to high, 1–3
Political interest, Q13	12,460	4.39	1.90	Low to high, 1–7
Young (under 30), Q2	12,694	0.17	0.38	Age < 30 = 1, else = 0
Older (over 64), Q2	12,694	0.14	0.35	Age > 64 = 1, else = 0
Context variables				
Distance capital of country to Moscow	12,694	1729	467	Min. 1150, max. 2500
GDP per capita $, PPP 2022	12,694	41,111	8706	Min. 30,777, max. 53,613
Global warming annual temperature °C	12,694	1.39	0.29	Min 0.93, max. 1.85

For regression analyses, all variables recoded to a range from 0 to 1. Risks recoded big, fair amount 1; little or no risk, 0. No. of cases are lower as a result of cumulative missing values in the respective set of variables

Question number refers to the questionnaire which is posted online at: https://hdl.handle.net/10419/314935

Sources European Security Survey. Fieldwork: 29 November–18 December 2022; 12,685 respondents. See Giebler et al. (2022): https://www.scripts-berlin.eu/research/research-projects/Short-term-Projects/2022_FIFA_Qatar/index.html. Context variables Intergovernmental sources

GPSR Compliance

The European Union's (EU) General Product Safety Regulation (GPSR) is a set of rules that requires consumer products to be safe and our obligations to ensure this.

If you have any concerns about our products, you can contact us on ProductSafety@springernature.com

In case Publisher is established outside the EU, the EU authorized representative is:

Springer Nature Customer Service Center GmbH
Europaplatz 3
69115 Heidelberg, Germany

Batch number: 08353780

Printed by Printforce, the Netherlands